TAKING CHARGE

A practical guide to
living with a disability
or health condition

First edition
January 2015

Taking charge
A practical guide to living with a disability or health condition

ISBN 978-1-9033-3566-6
© Disability Rights UK 2015

Published by Disability Rights UK.
Registered Charity No. 1138585

Design: © Anderson Fraser Partnership, London
Printed & bound by:
Stephens & George Print Group, Merthyr Tydfil

We hope you find this book useful. We welcome feedback on this and all our products so if you have any suggestions for change, for example, new content, please email feedback@disabilityrightsuk.org.

Disability Rights UK
CAN Mezzanine, 49-51 East Road, London N1 6AH

Tel: 020 7250 8181
www.disabilityrightsuk.org

Editor:
Liz Sayce OBE

Author:
Agnes Fletcher

Contributors:
Sue Bott
Stephen Brookes
Ken Butler
Philip Connolly
Sarah Cosby
Cheryl Gowar
Ian Greaves
Ben Kersey
Chris Ratcliffe
Robbie Spence
Tony Stevens

Production:
Anderson Fraser: Deb Kamofsky,
Paul McKenzie and Humphrey Weightman

Image credits:
David Baird (page 185)
Richard Brattan, Advance (pages 26, 27 and 93)
Dick Makin Imaging
Disabled Persons Railcard (pages 131, 191)
Eldon Associates Ltd (page 23)
IWC Media (page 43)
Motability (pages 132, 134 and 182)
Nordoff Robbins (page 189)
Regional Centre for Learners with Autistic Spectrum Disorders, City College Norwich (page 150)
VisitBritain/Pawel Libera

Thanks to:
Laurence Clark and Adele Hoskison-Clark
English Federation of Disability Sport
Norah Fry Research Centre (University of Bristol) and the Working Together with Parents Network (Jack's Story, pages 44/45)
Cathy and Thomas Pettigrew
Smriti Singh

Contents

Introduction

LIVING WITH DISABILITY

Nearly all of us are touched by disability or health conditions at some point in our lives. One in five of us has a long-term impairment or health condition that would be considered a 'disability' under the legislation that protects us from discrimination.

Nothing quite prepares you for the impact on your family of suddenly acquiring an impairment or health condition

As we get older, age-related health issues can start to affect our lives. Add to that our involvement with family members, older relatives, friends and colleagues living with disability and nearly all of us know something about the experience.

For many people it is only at 'turning points' that we have to deal with the impact on our own lives, for example:

- after an accident
- when we get a diagnosis (from multiple sclerosis to bi-polar disorder, epilepsy to dementia)
- when a child is born disabled or diagnosed with a serious health condition
- when a long-standing impairment enters a new phase
- when other circumstances change – from becoming a parent to more troubling issues like redundancy or bereavement.

At these times, life can seem strange and confusing. The life we know has suddenly changed.

"

The more easily people with disabilities can move around in public life, the less the chance they will be 'ghetto-ised' and seen as somehow separate from the rest of society. The more thought that goes into making places accessible, the less we need to ask others for help and the more we can regain our independence. Information is key and I hope this booklet helps.

Frank Gardner, BBC Security Correspondent, journalist and author

LIVE THE LIFE YOU CHOOSE

The good news is that many people come through this range of experiences with a satisfying and fulfilling life.

Life may not be as it was before, but as you go through your own process of change you find you can negotiate for changes that give you choice and control – and give you back the life you want.

Nobody can pretend that disability is an easy ride but shared experience and shared advice can lighten the burden immeasurably

It could be care or support at home, adjustments at work or a specific piece of equipment. You could be eligible for financial help to adapt your home or cover some additional day-to-day costs.

Deciding what will work for you depends on knowing what's possible and where to look for support and advice.

Knowing what you have a right to expect, and learning from the experiences of others are crucial for anyone living with disability and their families

Andrew Marr, journalist and author

This guide is designed to help. It lets you know what you have a right to expect from services and what other people in similar situations have found most useful.

It covers the resources and technology that may help you and includes details of many organisations that can provide specialist information, practical and legal advice.

It is rare and extremely valuable to have such a breadth of information available in one place. Access to clear, concise yet detailed information across a wide range of topics is an extremely powerful tool for people whose lives have been impacted by ill-health or disability. This guide covers some of the most important topics necessary to pursue an independent life.

David Blunkett

MAKE YOUR RIGHTS A REALITY

Everyone in the UK is protected by human, legal and consumer rights. If you have a 'disability' you have special rights, yet many people who could benefit, don't know about them or even consider themselves disabled.

Throughout the guide you will find summaries of human, legal and consumer rights legislation. We explain how these rights protect you in different situations at different times in your life, and equip you to put them into practice. And if you don't get what you need, or feel you are experiencing discrimination, we explain what action to take.

This guide is filled with stories from people in a whole range of situations who have made their rights work in practice and made the most of the resources available to lead independent lives.

Disability Rights UK campaigns on policy issues for rights in practice and provides expert advice and resources for disabled people, advisers and the organisations that support you.

We've produced this guide to help everyone with a health condition know what they have a right to expect in order to live a more independent life. It is packed with information that I hope you will find helpful.

Liz Sayce

Liz Sayce OBE, Chief Executive, Disability Rights UK

....

"

As a disabled parent and someone who navigates transport, employment and services on a daily basis, I know a lot about the barriers disabled people face – but also that there are often ways to overcome them.

Baroness Tanni Grey-Thompson

Planning your life

Health conditions and disability are part of human life. One in five of us – and pretty much every family – lives with some kind of disability or health condition. Whatever your experience, whether you were born with a condition or acquired it in later life, this book will help you lead the life you want.

. . . .

In this guide

This guide will help you put the building blocks in place for a good life. It lets you know what others going through similar challenges have found most useful; the support you should expect from social services, healthcare and the social security system; what is available in education and employment; how to access everything from travel to housing; and what tools and technologies can make life easier and more enjoyable.

This book is for people with any kind of health condition or disability – and many people have more than one. It is for you whether you have mobility difficulties, a mental health condition, a learning disability, a sensory impairment or long-term health condition. It may also be helpful to read if you support someone with a disability or health condition.

This first chapter gives you ideas about planning and managing a good life with a health condition or disability, for instance after an accident or diagnosis, or as life changes.

Later in the book you'll find chapters that deal with different areas of life:
- home
- family
- money
- technology and equipment
- health and social care services
- getting around
- learning and working
- leisure activities
- your rights.

Each chapter provides advice from others in similar situations for times when you don't get what you need or you feel you have been subject to discrimination. There is also a chapter that deals with this specifically.

Your rights

You have the right to a decent life, whatever your health or disability. This is enshrined in laws – from the United Nations Convention on the Rights of Persons with Disabilities to the Human Rights and Equality Acts.

A new life?

If you have recently developed a health condition or disability, your life may be changing in significant ways. This can be a challenge and take getting used to. If you have had a health condition or disability for a while, you may find that its impact changes when your circumstances change, for example as you get older, if the condition enters a new phase, if you start or finish work or there are changes in your family.

Huge developments in recent years have been led by people living with disabilities and health conditions, to forge ways to have the life we choose. Each person's journey through life's complexities is different, but there are common themes.

> "My panic does limit my daily activities but I work on improving my health and reducing the psychotropic drugs I am taking due to bothersome side effects, which I hate. I do things like meditate, yoga, light aerobic exercise 4-5 days per week, unless I feel really bad on a particular day. Life still has to go on and we do the best that we can."

Choice and control

The pioneers of 'independent living' showed that you can have choice, and control over your everyday life whatever the severity of your disability or health condition.

There is no need to give up on your ambitions or interests, to become 'just a patient' or to accept services if they don't support what you want to do with your life.

Many services now give you the option of a 'personal budget', which means you decide what type of health or social care suits you best, with information and learning from others who have tried things before you.

The independent living movement lays out the '12 pillars of independent living' – that together make up the foundations of a good life.

The 12 Pillars of Independent Living

1. Appropriate and accessible information.
2. An adequate income.
3. Appropriate and accessible health and social care provision.
4. A fully accessible transport system.
5. Full access to the environment.
6. Adequate provision of technical aids and equipment.
7. Availability of accessible and adapted housing.
8. Adequate provision of personal assistance.
9. Availability of inclusive education and training.
10. Equal opportunities for employment.
11. Availability of independent advocacy and self-advocacy.
12. Availability of peer counselling.

Use your new life as a reason to try new things. Get more involved with any grandkids you have or work with younger people as a volunteer. You'll learn a lot! If you can write, think about starting a blog. If you aren't great at computers and the internet, do a course.

Recovery

The 'recovery' movement has helped people come to terms with a changed life. It started with people with mental health difficulties – but it is relevant to everyone.

When you have a health condition or disability, you may feel "why me?". You may feel upset, angry or like giving up. Many of us feel this way: you have lost the life you thought you were going to have, and it can feel a bit like grieving. But you can get past that. Millions of people have.

In a weird way having a mental health problem actually helped me. It made me focused and dynamic. If I could cope with the voices in my head I could cope with anything.

Give yourself time. Consider talking to people who have been through something similar. Talk with a friend, family member or a health professional you trust and then concentrate on finding the things you want to do, even in changed circumstances.

ⓦ http://en.wikipedia.org/wiki/Recovery_approach

Whatever your situation, most people living with one or more health conditions or disabilities find that life is better if they take a pro-active approach to planning and managing their lives; feel they have the tools to negotiate for the things they need; and think through what they want to do with their lives.

It is possible to have the fulfilling life you want. It just may be different from the life you expected. You may need to do some things differently, to plan more (whether for each day or for the future) and to think carefully about how you use your resources. This includes your energy, your money and the support available from other people.

What do we mean by health conditions or disabilities?

Everyone will have their own ways of thinking about health conditions and disabilities.

At Disability Rights UK, we find that what can make the biggest difference to our experience of life is not just what health condition or disability we have but whether we get the support we want to live a good life and whether the world around us is inclusive.

So you may have some 'impairment' to the way you function at an individual level. Good healthcare and support, such as insulin for diabetes, can make a difference.

"I have an active life. Just because you are disabled, you don't have to sit there and wither and die. You have to keep active the best way you can. I don't feel sorry for myself. I deal with my disability. Some people who are disabled think their life is over. Well it isn't. Life goes on. Enjoy life to the best of your ability and live each day like it's your last."

You may find certain activities challenging – but this depends to a large extent on what resources, access and support you have.

For example, you may not be able to hear, but sign language interpretation can help you to communicate with people who don't use sign language. You may use a walking frame but ramps, handrails and lifts mean you can get access to your local cinema, to shops and other facilities you want to use.

What is disability? Am I 'disabled'?
'Disability' is used in different ways by different people and in different contexts. Many people tend to have quite a limited view of what it means – something related to wheelchairs or white sticks.

Equality law has a particular, broad definition of who is considered 'disabled'. Government disability benefits use a range of definitions to determine eligibility.

Some of the things that 'disability' or being a 'disabled person' can mean in official terms are having:
- a mobility or physical impairment, including dexterity or coordination difficulties
- a cognitive impairment: something you are born with, such as a learning disability caused by Down's syndrome, dyslexia or dyspraxia, or acquired such as a head injury or dementia
- a visual impairment
- a hearing impairment

You may face barriers in how and whether you do certain things, such as learning, working or sport – but this will usually depend upon the attitudes and environment you encounter.

For example, you may need time off work because of a fluctuating condition such as depression or multiple sclerosis and it will make a big difference if your employer is positive about making the job work for you.

- a mental health condition, such as schizophrenia, bipolar, anxiety or depression
- an atypical way of apprehending and communicating with the world, as a result of an autism spectrum condition
- a long-term health condition, such as diabetes, heart or lung dysfunction, cancer, Parkinson's disease or multiple sclerosis.

There are overlaps and these terms are not mutually exclusive. For example, someone with diabetes may have a visual impairment; someone with multiple sclerosis may experience mobility impairment.

Whether or not you choose to use any of these ways of describing yourself, this book is for you.

You can take charge of the words you use to describe your circumstances, just as you can take charge of other aspects of your life.

Creating your new life plan

Put simply, a life change associated with a health condition or disability can be a trigger for reviewing what you want from life. Many of us who are struggling with challenges of one kind or another spend a lot of time thinking "if only":

- "if only my health was better"
- "if only I had more money"
- "if only people would listen to what I want"
- "if only I had the energy, time or motivation to make the changes I know need making"
- "if only I was better at things".

The first step in creating a new life plan is to spend some time thinking through what you want, what is possible and what is needed to achieve what you want.

Disabled people are the best problem solvers. Baroness Campbell, disabled peer

WHAT DO I WANT OUT OF LIFE?

Consider things such as:

- Am I settled where I live? Where do I want to live and with whom?
- What do I want from relationships and/or family life?
- How do I want to make and interact with friends?
- What do I want to spend my days doing?
- What about work, learning and volunteering?
- What about leisure, being physically active, hobbies and community activities, such as religious observance, local clubs or volunteering?

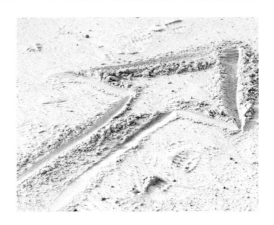

Julie Repper and Rachel Perkins say: "Everyone experiences the challenge of recovery at some point in life, for example when someone we love dies, or when we experience losses, traumas, illness or injuries. Recovery is a process of healing physically and emotionally, of adjusting one's attitudes, feelings, perceptions, beliefs, roles and goals in life. It is a painful process, yet often one of self-discovery, self-renewal and transformation. Recovery involves creating a new personal vision of oneself."

WHAT'S POSSIBLE?

- Can I do all the things that I want?
- Some things may look difficult given your disability – but don't assume they are impossible. With some adjustments or support you may be able to do more of the things you want.
- Some things may be impossible, some possible with help, some possible now but not in the future, some not possible now but perhaps in the future.
- What are my priorities? What choices or compromises do I want to make to move forward?

WHAT DO I NEED TO ACHIEVE THE THINGS I WANT?

- What information do I need (are there hearing loops, is there level access, can I have regular breaks from work – and many other specifics depending on your situation)?
- Support with my physical and/or mental health?
- Support with personal care, around my home, to be mobile?
- Equipment and technology?
- Support to access what I want? Such as using my rights or advocacy and support from others?

Pat Deegan, US advocate of mental health 'recovery' says: "Everyone's journey of recovery is unique. Each of us must find our own way and no one can do it for us ... Recovery is a process, not an end-point or a destination. Recovery is an attitude, a way of approaching the day and the challenges I face ... I know I have certain limitations and things I can't do. But rather than letting these limitations be occasions for despair and giving up, I have learnt that in knowing what I can't do, I also open up the possibilities of all I can do."

It's your life. Once you have decided on priorities there are several planning tools that may help you plan in detail:

A recovery plan
Ⓦ www.choicesinrecovery.com/about/ recovery-plan

A personal care plan
Ⓦ www.disabilityrightsuk.org/ managing-your-personal-budget

Practical support can make all the difference
SUPPORT SERVICES

Often, practical help with day-to-day tasks is what makes it possible for you to take part in family life and community.

Your disability may entitle you to state-funded practical support from health and/or social care services. This might include special equipment, adaptations to your home, help with things such as shopping, cleaning and dealing with personal care, telecare, support with your education or employment.

If you are entitled, you may have a 'personal budget' for health or social care which gives you choice about the support that would make most difference to you.

Your first step is to talk to your GP or ask your local council to arrange a health and social care assessment. In some cases, you will be visited by an occupational therapist and receive a written care plan stating what you're entitled to.

The personal budgets in health and social care help many of us to manage our care in a way that suits us, using a care plan drawn up with social services and/or an NHS health team. Many people find this provides a better quality of life – as you can choose the support that suits you best.

Focusing on things I can do and not getting caught up in what I can't do helps work towards recovery

There may be an organisation in your area run by people living with disability or health conditions. These organisations can be invaluable for peer support and learning about what is available locally, how useful it is and how it works.

There is more about help to promote your independence and participation in the chapter on health and social care.

HELP WITH YOUR FINANCES

Acquiring a health condition or disability may affect your income.

You may need time off work in the short or long term or may need to work part-time. But don't assume you can't work: many people find that with some adjustments (like changing your working hours, or help with travelling) they can work successfully.

Keeping in work can help you sustain income and social contact. There is strong evidence that work has positive health benefits.

See the chapter on employment for help on offer to stay in or get back into work.

If you are out of work for a while, you may be able to access help to find a job and to claim Employment Support Allowance or other benefits.

See the chapter on money for details.

Disability is also likely to mean an increase in the cost of day-to-day life. You could be entitled to financial support to meet these extra costs.

This could include:
- Personal Independence Payment (gradually replacing Disability Living Allowance) if you're under 65 and have costs associated with personal care or mobility.
- Attendance Allowance if you're over 65.

You can use a personal health budget to pay for a wide range of services, including therapies, personal care and equipment. This will allow you more choice and control over the health services and care you receive.

Through the direct payments scheme, you can get money from the local council to fund the support you need at home, including employing your own care assistants rather than relying on the council to arrange it for you. This gives you more control over the help and equipment you receive.

You could also be entitled to VAT relief on products and services associated with your disability, as well as lower council tax. There are also schemes that offer discounts – or free places for a carer – that operate on railways, buses, some cinemas and sports venues.

There is more information on these later in the book.

You can find comprehensive, up-to-date details of all social security benefits in Disability Rights UK's *Disability Rights Handbook,* available to order from our online shop:
Ⓦ www.disabilityrightsuk.org

Dealing with new challenges

You may face new challenges in how you do ordinary things, such as work, learn, shop, take exercise or participate in community activities.

There are huge numbers of organisations that can help you. Spend some time on the internet looking for sources of information and support. This guide gives you some starting points. For example, the English Federation of Disability Sport shows that you don't need to stop taking part in physical activity and exercise.

In 2009, 17-year-old David Allen from Sheffield successfully challenged a high street bank for breaking discrimination laws by failing to provide wheelchair access to his local branch.

The bank claimed that other branches were accessible and that they had offered Mr Allen telephone or internet banking. The judge criticised the bank for causing the teenager embarrassment, awarded £6,500 in compensation and ordered the bank to install a platform lift.

"I only wanted them to comply with the law and provide disabled access so I could get into my bank like my friends" says David.

The case set a clear precedent to businesses and service providers that they had to make 'reasonable adjustments' to give customers access.

The chapter on your rights will further explain using the rights that you have to negotiate for what you want and need.

Your rights

It's against the law for anyone to discriminate against you because of your health condition or disability. You're entitled to fair treatment in the workplace when it comes to recruitment, promotion, pay and when buying things or using services. Both employers and providers of services need to make changes to the way they do things to ensure you can do what you need to do.

Take charge of living well
WHETHER OR NOT YOU 'GET BETTER' YOU CAN HAVE A GOOD LIFE

When people are first diagnosed or injured, they often focus on 'getting better'. For some people, that is what happens – if, say, they break their leg. The reality for most of us with a long-term health condition or disability is that its impact changes our lives and also that the condition varies from day to day and month to month.

Of course it's important to access good healthcare that's appropriate to your condition but just as important is to plan for the life you want to have, the things you want to do, the people you want to see. Having that as a focus will help you to make the best of the health you have and the circumstances in which you find yourself.

Everyone faces challenges in life. How big or difficult these challenges are is different for each of us and varies through our lives. Managing a disability or health condition, which can mean managing lots of systems and bureaucracy to access what we need, can leave us feeling drained or struggling to cope. Often, we don't realise our own strengths – we are coping, even when it is a struggle.

I now control my panic attacks, rather than them controlling me and I live life to the full.

But most of us want to do more than cope and survive. While it may seem that leading a good life depends more on others than ourselves (and this guide is designed to support you in negotiating for what you need), there is good evidence that doing some simple things ourselves can make us feel happier and more satisfied with our lives.

For everyone, our well-being is improved by being able to:
- express what we think, feel and want
- make decisions about our lives, day to day
- keep in touch with friends and loved ones
- ask for help when we need it
- take a break from our usual routines from time to time
- do something we are good at and enjoy
- accept and be accepted by others for who we are
- support and care for others, whether that is in practical ways or by listening for them and expressing affection
- keep active
- eat well and drink sensibly.

Taking charge

Planning
- Do your research. Understand as much as you can about your situation and the resources available. Find information and organisations that can offer support or advice.
- Learn about the systems that may provide support. If you will need ongoing healthcare, find out what you're entitled to and how the NHS works. This includes waiting times and access to particular medicines and therapies. Get your GP, consultant and local pharmacist on your side.
- Keep good records and copies of paperwork. This is particularly important if you apply for social security benefits or don't get what you are entitled to.
- Know your rights. Are you entitled to compensation as a result of an injury? Or paid time off work to get used to a new condition? A basic understanding of the laws can protect you from discrimination and help you get what you are entitled to.
- Learn to be proactive and assertive. When faced with challenges, you may feel angry, frustrated or too timid to stand up for yourself. If you need or want something, think about who makes the decision. What will work best to persuade them? If you are struggling, get help from someone who can talk to people, write letters and argue your case with you.

Sharing experiences and ideas

'Peer support' is the help and support that people with a health condition or disability are able to give to one another. It may be social, emotional or practical support.

Often this happens through organisations focussed nationally or locally on a particular health condition or disability. Sometimes it happens through local disabled people's organisations.

Sometimes, we may not feel like spending time with others with similar experiences. We may want to feel 'normal'. That's fine – but many thousands of people have found that spending time with people who have 'been there' helps them to feel less alone or gives them useful tips on managing their lives better.

Disability can arise in a number of ways but the huge psychological impact should never be neglected. Often, newly disabled people shy away from organisations that might help them. But contact with people who face similar challenges is really important.

Taking charge

This book is designed to help you plan, manage and most of all enjoy the life you have, with one or more health conditions or disabilities.

Some people may view your life in negative or tragic terms. This is a common response to those of us who face health challenges. However, many thousands of people with significant physical, mental, sensory and cognitive challenges are living good lives, the lives we want, and have taken charge of bringing that about, with support from others where needed. You can do it too.

If you are not currently in contact with organisations that could offer peer support, think about it. You'll find contact details for various organisations here:

- Ⓦ www.disabilityrightsuk.org/membership/our-current-members
- Ⓦ www.ukdpc.net/site/current-members
- Ⓦ www.gov.uk/government/publications/disabled-peoples-user-led-organisations-list-and-contacts

At home

There is a huge range of housing options including buy or rent, flats or houses, sharing or on your own – some with various forms of support. For many people choosing where to live has nothing to do with any health condition or disability you may be experiencing. Others will make housing choices because of the way in which particular places, types of home and forms of support make a difference to their lives.

This chapter explores options that may be available to you, from staying in your own home to moving into specialised accommodation.

Where and how to live

They say that home is where the heart is. But the same home may not suit us throughout our lives, because of its structure and design or because of other factors that affect our wellbeing, such as whether:

- we have our own tenancy or mortgage
- we feel safe and connected to our neighbours and community
- we can use local facilities easily.

If you are considering a move, think about location first: where are your social networks, where do you feel safe and part of a community and how comfortable will you be getting out and about and using local facilities? Are there shops, cashpoints, work and leisure opportunities within easy reach? What are the local council's policies that particularly affect you if you have a health condition or disability?

You may be at a point in your life where you are thinking about whom you want to live with and any support you may need. Will you live alone or in shared housing, with family, a partner or friends?

Wherever you live, there are a range of things that can make you more independent and better able to do the things you want to.

Remember, you have the same right as anyone else to live where you want to and to take part in your local community.

Could I live here? Can I do the things I want to here? Do I feel safe and comfortable with my neighbours and the community? The answer in this house is: yes I can.

If you are thinking about moving because you need some support, first consider whether it would work to get what you need in your current home. Some people find that making some adaptations and getting some help from social care services is the right answer for them (see the chapter on health and social care).

"My mother had vascular dementia and was just managing at home, with some support from a social care agency to help her with shopping and cooking. Then she had a stroke which left her physically and mentally very frail. The hospital told her she needed to go into a nursing home.

Although confused, she was clear that she wanted to live at home. The family supported her to get what she wanted. She used the money that would have gone on the nursing home for a live-in carer at home. And being in her own home, where everything was familiar, helped her with the confusion. She had a good period of life with support at home, including celebrating her 90th birthday, and continued contact with neighbours and friends nearby."

Home adaptations

Most areas of the UK have a home improvement service to help people with health conditions and disabilities with repairs and small adaptations like grab rails. They can also help get grants for bigger adaptations. Many also offer 'handyperson services' to do small jobs, put in safety features and make sure homes are suitable after a spell in hospital. To find a local home improvement service contact:

Foundations
Bleaklow House, Howard Town Mill, Glossop SK13 8HT
Ⓣ 0845 864 5210
Ⓔ info@foundations.uk.com
Ⓦ www.foundations.uk.com/home

MAJOR ADAPTATIONS
Disabled Facilities Grants
For major adaptations such as installing a downstairs shower room, wider doorways or an adapted kitchen, you could apply to your local council for a Disabled Facilities Grant.

If you are a homeowner or tenant with a health condition or disability, or a landlord of a tenant with a health condition or disability you may be able to get a grant for adaptations needed to:
- make it easier to get into and out of the home – for example, by widening doorways or installing a ramp
- improve access between the house and the garden, yard or balcony
- ensure the safety of people living in the home – for example, by improved lighting or providing a specially adapted room where someone can be left unattended

- improve or provide a suitable heating system and adapt heating and lighting controls to make them easier to use
- improve access to your living room and bedroom
- make it easier to prepare and cook food
- provide or improve access to the kitchen, toilet, washbasin and bath or shower – for example, by installing a stairlift or downstairs bathroom
- improve access and movement around the home so that someone can care for another resident, such as a child or partner.

Lifetime Homes

Lifetime Homes is a design concept that aims to make new housing accessible for disabled people and easy to adapt to meet future requirements. It consists of 16 design standards that can be universally applied to new homes. Many local planning policies already require the Lifetime Homes standards in new developments. In Wales and Northern Ireland, complying with the standards is a legal requirement.

The scheme is administered and supported by Habinteg Housing, which encourages all social housing providers and private builders to use the standards.

Lifetime Homes' design standards include:
- level entry to the main entrance or a suitable alternative

Living in a Lifetime Home

Jason and his two children moved to a Lifetime Home. "It's just made my life that much easier. Having an accessible house at ground level helps with getting Joshua in and out of his wheelchair. We have a downstairs wet room and shower for him and are just about to have a stairlift fitted so that I don't have to carry him up and downstairs. My children have got their own space in this house and everything we need for Joshua is here. There should be more Lifetime Homes."

- an entrance door wide enough to let a wheelchair through
- a toilet on the entrance level that is capable of having a shower installed
- adequate circulation and door widths in the entrance floor
- switches, sockets and other controls at appropriate heights
- a level or gently sloping path from a nearby parking space to the entrance
- a lift of appropriate size in blocks of flats
- walls and ceilings to which handrails and hoists can be fitted in bathrooms and bedrooms
- an area that could be used as a bedroom on the entrance floor
- staircase that could take a stairlift or space for a through-the-floor lift.

For more information on the scheme:
Ⓦ www.lifetimehomes.org.uk

The Disabled Facilities Grant is normally paid by your local council (or your local housing executive grants office if you are in Northern Ireland) who will give you an application form. You can apply for a grant for someone else who has a health condition or disability if you clearly state this on your application form.

To approve a grant, the council must be satisfied that the works are necessary and appropriate for your needs, as well as being reasonable and practicable in relation to the property.

You will usually be assessed by an occupational therapist, who will make a recommendation to the housing grants officers.

Other financial help

If you are awarded a Disabled Facilities Grant but the grant is not enough to cover the cost of the work you need, you may get help under other housing grant or payment schemes.

Housing authorities have the power to provide discretionary help that might be used to top up a Disabled Facilities Grant or to help you move if that would be a better option. For private householders help may be provided through low-cost loans or equity release schemes.

Council social care departments can sometimes provide equipment and adaptations costing up to £1000 without charge, or loan equipment such as stairlifts.

You are entitled to a decision within six months of your application date. Your housing authority cannot refuse to let you make an application. The maximum grant payable is currently £30,000 in England, £25,000 in Northern Ireland and £36,000 in Wales.

A separate system operates through Housing Grants in Scotland. For information visit the *Housing* section of:
Ⓦ www.adviceguide.org.uk/scotland

If the grant is for the benefit of a child with a health condition or disability, the amount of money you earn and any savings that you have will not be taken into account. For applications from or on behalf of adults with health conditions or disabilities, the amount will depend on the income and savings that you and your partner have.

Having building work done

If you are applying for a Disabled Facilities Grant, do not have any work carried out until your application has been approved. If the work is urgent, contact your council.

Whether or not you are paying for the work yourself or through a Disabled Facilities Grant, check whether you need planning permission first.

Many common building works and extensions will not need permission but you must check with the council. You or your builder will also need to ensure that the work complies with building regulations. If it is a major project, use a qualified architect or surveyor to prepare the plans and supervise the work.

Check the reputation of builders and contractors and ensure they are members of a trade association that provides a guarantee or arbitration service, for example the Federation of Master Builders or National Federation of Builders.

ⓦ www.fmb.org.uk

ⓦ www.builders.org.uk

Find out if your local council has a list of local architects and builders who have experience of carrying out similar adaptations.

VAT on building work

Some building work to adapt existing housing for an occupant with a health condition or disability may be zero-rated for VAT.

This includes:
- building ramps or widening doorways or passages
- extending or adapting a bathroom or toilet
- installing a lift
- putting in an alarm system to call for help.

The contractor or supplier should know whether the work is zero-rated. Information is available in VAT Notice 701/7, available from HM Revenue and Customs (HMRC).

You can get more advice on VAT on building work from HMRC, online at www.gov.uk or from your council, a housing advice centre, a home improvement agency or Citizens Advice.

Energy saving

There are lots of things you can do to save money on your utility bills. Check for deals and compare suppliers. Some energy companies and local councils offer free insulation to some people. For some properties this can make a huge difference to your bills.

The Green Deal can also help you make energy-saving improvements to your home and find the best way to pay for them. Improvements depend on your home. Examples include:
- cavity wall or loft insulation
- heating
- draught-proofing, double-glazing
- renewable energy generation – such as solar panels or heat pumps.

To find out more:
ⓦ www.gov.uk/green-deal-energy-saving-measures/overview

Green Deal

You may be eligible for a Green Deal loan to finance energy-saving improvements to your home.

 All Green Deal organisations must be authorised – look for the quality mark.

The Green Deal isn't available in Northern Ireland but other schemes or grants may be available.

You can find a Green Deal company and check they are an authorised assessor, provider or installer at:
ⓦ http://gdorb.decc.gov.uk

COULD YOUR HOME BENEFIT?

There are various ways to check if your property could benefit from energy-saving improvements:

Use an online tool, such as the Stroma certification tool:
- Ⓦ www.stroma.com/certification/the-green-deal/green-deal-for-customers

Use the energy grants calculator:
- Ⓦ www.gov.uk/energy-grants-calculator

Talk to a Green Deal assessor or provider:
- Ⓦ http://gdorb.decc.gov.uk/consumersearch

For free, impartial advice on energy saving in your home and cutting your fuel bills contact:

Energy Saving Advice Service (England and Wales)
- Ⓣ 0300 123 1234
  Monday to Friday, 9am to 8pm, Saturday, 10am to 2pm.

Home Energy (Scotland)
- Ⓣ 0808 808 2282
  Monday to Friday, 8am to 8pm, Saturday, 9am to 5pm.
- Ⓦ www.energysavingtrust.org.uk

Smart homes

When you're not at home, nagging little doubts can start to crowd your mind. Did I turn the iron off? Did I set the security alarm? Are the kids doing their homework or watching television?

With a smart home, you can get rid of these worries with a quick glance at your smart phone or tablet. You can connect the devices and appliances in your home so they can communicate with each other and with you.

Any device in your home that uses electricity can be put on your home network and be at your command. Whether you give that command by voice, remote control, tablet or smart phone, the home reacts. Most applications relate to lighting, home security, home entertainment and thermostat regulation.

Technology at home
"I work in tech so I'm really into new developments. Like most of us, disability touches my family in various ways.

My dad is on his own now mum's gone and he has memory problems. I've got him some kit that means I can check that the temperature in his house is set right for winter or summer – he was struggling to remember how to alter it and I've come in to find him freezing cold. Of course, I thought about him moving in with us – but he says he wants to stay where he is as long as he can.

Also, my son has some learning difficulties. He's 12 now and I want him to be more independent. He can use an ipad application so I set him up with apps so he could put the TV and music on himself. He's really chuffed."

Smart homes and home automation are becoming more common and they have great potential to help people with health conditions and disabilities ranging from dyspraxia, learning disabilities and dementia through to tetraplegia.

Smart home technology can help with basic domestic tasks, such as running the washing machine, closing the curtains, keeping track of what food you need. Many of us may soon have 'intelligent' fridges that tell internet supermarkets to deliver what we need. If you are arriving back from a few days away on a cold evening, you'll be able to set the thermostat remotely.

Buying or renting your own home

If you're considering buying a new home, it is worth:

- checking the accessibility standards it is built to
- contacting the developer to see if they can incorporate design features that you need.

All new homes must be built to standards that enable wheelchair users and people with mobility impairments to visit and have access to an entry level living space and toilet. An increasing number of homes (mainly social housing) are built to the Lifetime Homes standards.

If your home needs to be wheelchair accessible – with the necessary circulation space and level access in all parts of the home it's worth checking with local housing associations.

Also look at a web resource called Accessible Property Register, which provides information on accessible and adapted housing for sale or rent (see the useful contacts at the end of this chapter).

Disability Rights UK is pressing for more wheelchair accessible housing and for a national accessible housing register, updated by all local authorities and landlords.

Help to Buy

You may be able to get financial help through this government home ownership scheme if you live in England and can't afford to buy a home. Different schemes operate in Scotland, Wales and Northern Ireland.

Ⓦ www.gov.uk/affordable-home-ownership-schemes

Home Buy

This is a government scheme that offers financial support and assistance to qualifying first-time buyers, key workers (such as teachers and nurses) and social tenants.

Ⓦ www.homebuyservice.co.uk

Housing registers

If you can't afford to buy or rent privately, and you have a low income, contact your local council about going on the housing register. This is a list of people who want to rent council or housing association properties.

Since there are more people in need than there are homes available, councils have to prioritise. Anyone who needs to move for health or access reasons should get priority – but check your council's policies on this.

In England, many councils have adopted 'choice-based lettings', which mean people on the housing register are not offered a particular property but are invited to bid for any available property they think meets their needs. Properties with access features should be flagged up. Whose bid is successful depends on who has the highest priority need.

In some areas you can get advice from a dedicated 'disabled person's housing service'. In others an accessible housing register provides up-to-date details of accessible or adapted homes available for renting.

Councils have powers to pay a relocation grant to help someone with the cost of moving to a home that is already more accessible or could be made so more easily.

Housing associations

Housing associations are non-profit organisations providing rented homes or help for people on low incomes to buy a home.

Some operate on a local or regional basis and others specialise in providing housing for people with particular housing needs, such as supported housing. Some housing associations have their own waiting lists so it is worth contacting them as well.

Most vacancies in housing association properties are allocated to people nominated by the local council. However, depending on their individual policies, associations may also accept applications from individuals or other organisations.

Taking charge

Where you live
It might not be possible to find your ideal home but, if you are clear about what is most important for you, it will be easier to make decisions about the options open to you. When thinking about where you might live, consider:

- what facilities you need or want, for example, a garden or a downstairs loo
- the size and type of accommodation, for example, flat, house, newbuild, top floor or ground floor
- the location: close to shops, close to public transport, near to where you work or with good transport links, close to a park, quiet, etc.
- who you want to live with: your partner, a son or daughter, with lots of other people or alone
- what you can afford to pay
- what local rates of housing benefit are available.

Taking charge at home

Martyn Coutts is delighted by the stability that his own home has given him. He now works alongside his former advocate, speaking up on behalf of other people with learning disabilities.

Martyn has Asperger's syndrome and a learning disability. He says that before he moved into his own place he lacked the self-confidence to work with advocacy charity Cornwall People First. He is understandably very proud of his role: "My advocate was helping me; now she's my colleague. I work one day a week. I hope it is helping other people with learning disabilities."

Before moving into his two-bedroom flat in Saltash, Martyn was living with his parents and twin sisters. Being at home was a double-edged sword. While Martyn and his family felt it was safer, he also felt dependent on his parents and lacking in purpose.

"I wanted my own space and to be more independent; living at home was making me feel claustrophobic, as if I was tucked away in one corner of the house. I felt I wasn't doing anything or going anywhere with my life."

Martyn says that the move left him "nervous but excited" and within a couple of weeks he began referring to the flat as "home".

"The town's nearby, which is useful for shopping and it's easy to get about. The thing that caught my eye was the view of the Royal Albert Bridge and I liked the front room and space in the garden."

Achieving his dream of living alone also gave Martyn the confidence to stop a voluntary gardening role with a local charity, which he had been doing for a couple of years. Although he had enjoyed it, he felt it was not leading anywhere.

Martyn has 10 hours a week personal assistant support funded by Cornwall County Council but says home ownership has boosted his independence enormously. He has recently started driving lessons.

"I still struggle a bit with the social side of things but I do know my neighbours and I do my own cooking. I feel I can look after myself rather than just helping mum."

Not long after moving in, Martyn got a cat, Bailey, and he has become a keen amateur photographer. He says: "The future? It's good. It's looking really good."

From *Space to live* published by Advance with Disability Rights UK:
Ⓦ www.advanceuk.org

Some associations operate partnership schemes with voluntary bodies where they provide the housing and the partner provides an agreed level of care or support for tenants.

Shared ownership

Housing associations often run shared ownership schemes where you part-buy and part-rent a home. You might buy a 25%, 50% or 75% share in your home and pay rent on the share that you don't buy. For information visit
Ⓦ www.shared-ownership.org.uk

Several models have developed to meet the needs of different people. The current model that works best for people with health conditions and disabilities is called HOLD (home ownership for people with long-term disabilities).

Over the last 15 years, more than 1600 disabled people have moved into shared ownership housing schemes. Shared ownership offers control and choice over where a person lives and who supports them in their home. Under shared ownership the housing is totally independent from an individual's support package, so even if their support needs change their housing can remain constant.

Shared ownership works well for many people because it:
- promotes a long-term housing option
- incorporates choice and control over where a person lives
- builds confidence and self-esteem
- reduces the stigma associated with being in 'specialist' housing
- encourages independence.

Shared ownership is the best thing ever for my son. It has changed not only his life but also our lives. Dawn Coutts

"We've both got mobility and health challenges. My husband has had hip replacements, knee operations and a blood clot. I've got spondylosis, a spine condition, which limits my mobility. Where we were before was unsuitable after my husband's blood clot. It was built after the second world war for returning soldiers, with small rooms and lots of stairs – and it had a huge garden. Maintaining the garden and having to go up and down stairs all the time was tough. Our new house is so easy to manage – wide doors, plenty of storage and a large kitchen – far less scope for accidents. We'll stay here now – whatever happens with our health, we're in the very best place to manage."

Supported living

Supported living can be a good option if you need some help with personal care. You can rent accommodation suitable to your disability or health needs and at the same time have access to 24-hour care and support. Supported living enables you to live in your own accessible home while being in control and independent.

There are supported living properties across the UK, with many close to town centres, so it is easy to visit shops and have a social life.

Supported living suits a wide range of people. In recent years, many local authorities have changed services from residential care to supported housing particularly for people with learning disabilities. An important outcome of supported living can be being able to achieve choice, control and community inclusion.

Sheltered accommodation

Sheltered housing (sometimes referred to as retirement housing) is aimed at people over 60 years old, although some schemes are available to over-55s.

They are self-contained, purpose-built flats, houses or bungalows with their own front door, kitchen and bathroom. They are available to couples or single people and offer independent living with extra help if needed.

As a resident, you can come and go as you please, and usually only need to inform the scheme manager if you intend to be away overnight or won't be in when they are due to visit.

The facilities available vary depending on the individual scheme. Some have restaurants and guest rooms for family and friends. Many have communal areas such as a laundry room, lounge and gardens and provide residents with opportunities for socialising with each other and the wider community.

They are run by scheme managers or wardens who may live on site or work office hours. The scheme manager is there to help arrange suitable support for residents, manage any repair work on the properties, and help out in emergencies. They can focus on residents' wellbeing, get to know them and listen to their concerns but they don't provide personal care services or administer medication.

Residents also have access to 24-hour emergency care assistance via an alarm system linked to a monitoring centre, which will contact a family member, GP or emergency service if needed.

Taking charge at home
"After my husband died I moved into sheltered housing following my second hip replacement, which didn't go so well.

My son works for a housing charity. He made me push for a secure tenancy, which gives me the peace of mind of knowing that I can stay here as long as I want.

Even if I need more support they can't boot me out! And nor should they be able to – this is my home."

ELIGIBILITY

Most sheltered housing properties are rented from local councils or housing associations. There is a high demand for these homes and some will have waiting lists. Applicants often have to meet eligibility criteria to qualify. You will usually need to show that:

- your current home doesn't meet your needs
- you have a medical or social need to move, such as a health condition or disability or a need to be nearer your family
- you are unable to buy a property yourself and need to rent instead.

If you are an existing council or housing association tenant, you would need to speak to your landlord about transferring to sheltered accommodation.

To apply for sheltered accommodation run by your local council, contact its housing department. There is a search facility available on the GOV.UK website to help you find contact details for local sheltered and supported housing.

Ⓦ www.gov.uk/apply-for-sheltered-housing

To apply for sheltered housing run by a housing association you either need to be referred to a particular housing association by your local council or approach the housing association yourself to find out about availability.

Try to arrange for a secure tenancy if you don't own the new property. This means that you won't be obliged to move if your needs change.

EXTRA COSTS TO RESIDENTS

As well as rent or mortgage, you will usually have to pay a monthly service charge to help cover the cost of the scheme manager and maintenance of communal areas.

Ask the scheme manager how much the service charge is for the accommodation you are considering, and check what is and isn't included before you choose a particular scheme.

Private developments

Some private developers have sheltered housing properties that you can buy or part-buy through shared ownership schemes. These are advertised on the open market and are usually sold as leasehold properties. Some private developers also rent out these properties.

For information on private providers of sheltered accommodation contact Elderly Accommodation Counsel:
Ⓦ www.eac.org.uk

Or First Stop
Ⓣ 0800 377 7070
Ⓦ www.firststopcareadvice.org.uk

WHAT YOU NEED TO CONSIDER

Moving into sheltered housing may offer more security and support than your current accommodation. However, it will involve moving out of your existing home and possibly living in a smaller space.

When looking for a suitable scheme, think about the style of the accommodation on offer, the quality of facilities, and the location of the site. Visit the scheme you are considering and speak to the manager and some of the residents before making a decision.

> The Elderly Accommodation Counsel has developed a quality mark to encourage scheme managers to provide detailed information about their facilities to potential residents.

Age UK offers advice on what to think about when deciding whether to move into sheltered accommodation. Visit *Housing choices* in the Home and care section of their website:
ⓦ www.ageuk.org.uk

Your rights

You have a right to a private and family life under the Human Rights Act. This means that you can't be made to live apart from a partner against their and your wishes.

Residential care

Most people want to stay in their own homes and can do so with the right support. Don't assume just because others are suggesting it that you have to leave your home because of a health condition or disability. Even if it is professionals or family members who are suggesting it, because it might seem safer or cheaper, it is your choice. No one should have to live somewhere they haven't chosen.

Some people do feel that one of the many types of residential care is right for them. Residential care facilities may be privately owned, or run by a charity or the local council. They include:

- residential care homes
- residential care homes with nursing care
- extra care housing
- retirement villages.

Deciding on a long-term stay in residential care is a significant decision financially, practically and emotionally. You will need to think about your own preferences and decide what services will meet your needs, now and in the future. It is not always an easy decision.

Independent advice can help you take all the important factors into account and make the right decision. Your council can tell you about local information services that can help you think through your options. Many local and national charities will also be able to provide information and advice.

Support for homeless people

If you are facing homelessness or have already left your home, you may have more rights than you think. If you're having difficulties paying for your accommodation, see the chapter on money.

HELP FROM SOCIAL CARE

The social care department of your local council has duties to help certain groups of people who become homeless. These include:

- people with health conditions and disabilities, including mental health problems
- older people
- most people under the age of 18
- people who have been in care (normally up to age 21 or up to the age of 25 if still in full-time education).

The council may also be able to help families with children if they are eligible for help. Get advice if you are in this situation or have problems getting help from the council.

There is helpful information in the *Get advice* section of Shelter's website:
ⓦ http://england.shelter.org.uk

Your rights

If you're homeless

- Even if you don't have a home you still have rights.
- If you are homeless the council has to give you advice and assistance.
- You still have the right to see a doctor, vote, and claim benefits.

RIGHTS TO STAY IN OR RETURN TO YOUR HOME

If you are asked to leave your home it is important to check if you have the right to remain. You may have the right to stay in your home:

- if your landlord tries to evict you without following the correct legal procedure
- after a relationship breakdown even if you are not the home-owner or tenant.

If you leave your home when you don't have to, or do not return when you have the right to, it could affect any right you may have to get homelessness help from the council. If possible, get advice before leaving.

Even if you have already left your home you may be able to return if you still have the right to live there. You may need legal advice from a housing adviser or lawyer.

Further information

Shelter provides advice and support about housing and homelessness. For more information about your housing rights visit the *Get advice* section of their website:
ⓦ http://england.shelter.org.uk/ get_advice

YOUR RIGHT TO EMERGENCY HOUSING

Local councils have specific legal duties towards homeless people. If any person who is homeless or threatened with homelessness approaches the council for help it has to provide them with advice and assistance.

Some people are also entitled to accommodation from the local council. You are entitled to emergency accommodation if the council believes you fit certain specific legal criteria.

To meet these you must be:
- eligible for assistance
- legally classed as homeless
- in priority need. This can include being 'vulnerable' because of a disability, mental health issue or learning difficulty.

If you are aged 16 or 17, you are normally entitled to housing and support from your local council. In most cases social care have responsibility for finding you somewhere to live:

If you are under 18
Young people under the age of 18 have different rights to benefits and different rights to accommodation if they become homeless. Your rights will also depend on whether you have spent time in care in the past.

If you are homeless and the council is refusing to help you, contact Civil Legal Advice. Their advisers can advise on the council's housing duties. You may be able to get help from their legal advisers if you qualify for legal help funding. Be prepared to answer questions about your income and savings so the helpline adviser can tell you if you qualify:
- Ⓦ www.gov.uk/civil-legal-advice

RIGHTS TO CLAIM BENEFITS
You are entitled to claim benefits. If you don't have a bank account, you can ask for a Simple Payment card.

Your benefits will be paid straight to this card, which you take to a PayPoint outlet displaying the Simple Payment sign (for example in newsagents, convenience stores and supermarkets) to collect your money.

You may also be able to apply for a grant or loan from your council's local welfare scheme. Your chances of getting support will depend on your situation and the amount of money the council has in its budget. You may also be eligible for a budgeting loan from the DWP if you are on certain benefits. For details see:
- Ⓦ http://england.shelter.org.uk/get_advice/money_problems/in_a_crisis

If you have lived abroad
People who have lived abroad have different housing and homeless rights. These depend on:
- when you entered the country
- the purpose of your stay (such as visitor, student, for work or marriage)
- whether you are seeking asylum
- whether you are a European Union or European Economic Area national.

You may need help from a specialist immigration adviser. See the *Housing rights for new arrivals* section of:
- Ⓦ www.housing-rights.info

For further information, call Shelter's free housing advice helpline on 0808 800 4444 or contact a local advice agency.

REGISTERING WITH A DOCTOR

You are entitled to register with a doctor. You can use a temporary address, such as a friend's place or a day centre. You can find a doctor in your area by visiting the *Services near you* section of the NHS Choices website.

ⓦ www.nhs.uk

There are also specialist medical centres for people who are homeless or roofless (sleeping rough).

THE RIGHT TO VOTE

You are entitled to vote if you are homeless (if you are a UK citizen over the age of 18). You can register at a temporary address or by making a 'declaration of local connection'. This is a statement that you make to the local electoral office to say where you spend most of your time. To find out more about how to register:

ⓦ www.aboutmyvote.co.uk/register-to-vote/how-to-register-to-vote

Taking charge

Harassment and hate crime

Some people with health conditions and disabilities experience negative attitudes from neighbours and others in their area. This can be distressing and frightening and you should seek help as soon as possible.

If you are in this situation, you should be able to get help from the police, your local disability organisation or the council. If you feel you or your property is in immediate physical danger, call the police straight away.

What is a hate crime?

A disability-related hate crime or incident is any incident which is perceived by the victim or any other person to be based upon prejudice towards or hatred of the victim because of their disability or perceived disability.

Having your property vandalised or marked with graffiti counts as disability-related harassment.

Other examples are being:

- verbally abused or sworn at
- intimidated
- harassed
- bullied
- physically abused.

Reporting hate crime

Disability hate crime is the most under-reported crime in the UK. Home Office figures suggest that up to 70,000 incidents a year happen in the UK whilst only about 2% ever get to the reporting stage.

But this is changing. Councils and the police are beginning to take individual incidents of harassment more seriously, preventing them escalating and improving prosecution rates.

How to report a hate crime

You'll find more on what to do if you experience hate crime or disability-related harassment, including a number of different ways to report the incident, in the chapter on your rights.

Useful contacts

Accessible Property Register
c/o Conrad Hodgkinson, 11 Stumperlowe Croft, Sheffield S10 3QW
📞 0774 911 9385
📧 conradh@accessible-property.org.uk
🌐 www.accessible-property.org.uk
The website has information on accessible and adapted housing for sale or rent, including both private and social housing. People looking for housing can place a 'Property Wanted' notice on the site.

Community Housing Cymru
2 Ocean Way, Cardiff CF24 5TG
📞 029 2067 4800
📧 enquiries@chcymru.org.uk
🌐 www.chcymru.org.uk
Represents housing associations and community mutuals in Wales. Members work closely with local government, third sector organisations and the Welsh Government to provide a range of social housing services in communities across Wales.

Counsel and Care
6 Avonmore Road, Kensington Olympia, London W14 8RL
📞 0845 300 7585
📧 advice@counselandcare.org.uk
🌐 www.counselandcare.org.uk
Provides information and advice for older people and their families and carers on residential and community care. Publishes guides and factsheets, downloadable from their website or available free of charge from the above address.

Habinteg Housing Association
Holyer House, 20-21 Red Lion Court, London EC4A 3EB
📞 01274 853 160 or 0845 606 2608
📧 info@habinteg.org.uk
🌐 www.habinteg.org.uk
A specialist provider of accessible housing, Habinteg provides over 2,000 homes across England, of which over a quarter are designed for wheelchair users and the rest to accessibility standards. They provide advice to other housing associations on disability equality policies. Sister organisations operate in Northern Ireland, Scotland, Wales and the Irish Republic.

Housing Options
Stanelaw House, Sutton Lane, Sutton, Witney OX29 5RY
📞 0845 456 1497
📧 enquiries@housingoptions.org.uk
🌐 www.housingoptions.org.uk
An advisory service for anyone concerned with housing for people with learning disabilities, their families and carers. The website includes a wide range of information sheets.

Joseph Rowntree Foundation
The Homestead, 40 Water End, York YO30 6WP
📞 01904 629 241;
    textphone 01904 615 910
📧 info@jrf.org.uk
🌐 www.jrf.org.uk
Supports a programme of research and development projects in housing, social care and social policy. Also carries out practical innovative projects in housing and care through the Joseph Rowntree Housing Trust, including the development of the concept of Lifetime Homes.

Livability
50 Scrutton Street, London EC2A 4XQ
- **T** 020 7452 2000
- **E** info@livability.org.uk
- **W** www.livability.org.uk

Delivers a wide range of services for disabled adults and children. They are a provider of care homes and nursing care to people with physical or learning disabilities. To find out more use the service finder on their website.

Mobility Friendly Homes
99 South Street, Eastbourne BN21 4LU
- **T** 0845 612 0280
- **E** info@mobilityfriendlyhomes.co.uk
- **W** www.mobilityfriendlyhomes.co.uk

An online estate agent for disabled people wanting to buy or rent an accessible or adapted property. It lists properties across the UK with details of access features and adaptations as well as other property details.

National Housing Federation
Lion Court, 25 Procter Street, London WC1V 6NY
- **T** 020 7067 1010
- **E** info@housing.org.uk
- **W** www.housing.org.uk

Provides information on housing associations and other independent social landlords and affordable housing providers in England. It has around 1,200 members who are responsible for 2.5 million homes.

Northern Ireland Federation of Housing Associations
6c Citylink Business Park, Albert Street, Belfast BT12 4HB
- **T** 028 9023 0446
- **W** www.nifha.org

Ownership Options in Scotland
The Melting Pot, 5 Rose Street, Edinburgh EH2 2PR
- **T** 0131 247 1400
- **E** info@housingoptionsscotland.org.uk
- **W** www.housingoptionsscotland.org.uk

A charity that provides information and advice to disabled people in Scotland to help them overcome the legal, financial and practical barriers to home ownership.

Scottish Federation of Housing Associations
3rd floor, Sutherland House, 149 St Vincent Street, Glasgow G2 5NW
- **T** 0141 332 8113
- **E** sfha@sfha.co.uk
- **W** www.sfha.co.uk

Shelter
88 Old Street, London EC1V 9HU
- **T** 0808 800 4444
- **E** info@shelter.org.uk
- **W** www.shelter.org.uk

The national housing and homelessness charity that campaigns for decent housing and helps people find and keep a home. It provides advice by telephone, through publications, on its website and through a network of housing advice centres around the country.

Your rights
THE EQUALITY ACT 2010

The Equality Act 2010 says that those who qualify as 'disabled people' under the Act (people with a wide range of health conditions and disabilities) should not be discriminated against in relation to renting or buying property.

For information about the Equality Act and how it applies to housing situations, visit the Equality and Human Rights Commission website:
Ⓦ www.equalityhumanrights.com

UN CONVENTION ON THE RIGHTS OF PERSONS WITH DISABILITIES

Article 19 of the UN Convention says that:

- Disabled people have an equal right to live in and take part in the community.
- Disabled people have the right to the same choice and control as non-disabled people.
- Governments should do everything they can to ensure disabled people enjoy these rights.

Governments should ensure that:

- Disabled people have the right to choose where they live and who they live with – no disabled person should be unlawfully forced into a particular living arrangement (for example be forced to live in a care home against their will).
- Disabled people have access to a wide range of support services (at home and in the community) including personal assistance to prevent isolation and support inclusion.
- Disabled people can access the same community services as everyone else.

Article 28 says that:

- Disabled people have the right to a good enough standard of living including clean water, decent clothes, enough food and a decent home. There should not be big gaps between disabled people's standard of living and non-disabled people's.
- Disabled people should expect to see continuous improvements in their standard of living.

Your family

For most of us relationships with family members are very important. They can be great, they can be challenging – whether it's our parents, children, siblings, nieces, nephews, grandchildren, uncles, aunts, grandparents or partners.

In most families, someone will experience a health condition or disability at some time. It's also quite common for a family to include more than one person with a health condition or disability. You might have a health condition yourself and be providing support to an older relative or have a child or grandchild who has a health condition or disability as well.

This chapter explores some of the challenges of family life if you have a disability or health condition

Romantic and sexual relationships

As someone with a disability or health condition, you have the same right as anyone else to establish a relationship, long-term partnership or marriage based on the wishes of both people.

HELP WITH SEXUAL RELATIONSHIPS

Many of us want a loving and/or sexual relationship with a partner. Some people experience challenges with sex because of mobility or physical difficulties; others because of the symptoms of a long-term health condition or the side-effects of medication, which can include fatigue, pain and nausea.

For people with transmissible conditions such as HIV and hepatitis, there can be additional difficulties.

What disabled people need is full and equal rights; an inclusive society, which doesn't create barriers. Forming sexual relationships, casual or committed, with mistakes, is part of that.

Penny Pepper, author of *Desires Reborn*, a fictional depiction of the relationships of a group of disabled characters

Fran Vicary, an advocate for the rights of people with disability says: "I have cerebral palsy from birth, and my physical disability means I cannot independently dress, shower, feed myself or do any fine motor tasks – but with support, I can have a fulfilling sexual life. I wish more people with a disability could say the same."

SEXUAL ORIENTATION AND DISABILITY/HEALTH

Sexual orientation is an enduring emotional, romantic, sexual or affectional attraction to another person.

It can be distinguished from other aspects of sexuality including biological sex, gender identity (the psychological sense of being male or female) and the social gender role (adherence to cultural norms for feminine and masculine behaviour).

Dr Daniel Atkinson, a GP who sits on the board of Outsiders, which supports disabled people with sexual issues, says: "Thinking about discussing sex is more frightening than actually doing it and the reactions we're fearful of very rarely occur".

Not talking about sexual symptoms during a consultation may not only be denying people support and help but also denying health professionals a full picture of the person's experience.

It's also very easy to underestimate the importance of sex. Sex or masturbation isn't just about offering a physical release. Sexual health is heavily intertwined with healthy self-esteem. As one Outsiders client says: "There is this overwhelming sense of achievement that I have somehow fulfilled my calling as a man and my self-esteem is lifted for a few important moments".

Sexual orientation exists along a continuum that ranges from being exclusively gay or lesbian (homosexual) to exclusively straight (heterosexual) and includes various forms of bisexuality, where someone is attracted to both their own sex and the opposite sex.

Sexual orientation is different from sexual behaviour, because it refers to feelings and identity not activity. Sometimes people are not able to express their sexual orientation through sexual behaviour, due to religious or cultural restrictions or barriers related to disability or health.

Prejudices, negative stereotypes and discrimination are deeply imbedded when it comes to disability and sexual activity, particularly same sex (gay or lesbian) sex.

Your rights

The UK has recently passed laws to ensure equality, whatever your sexual orientation. So if you are living with disability and you are gay or bisexual, no one should discriminate against you on either ground.

While this guide focuses primarily on taking charge in terms of a disability or health condition, and on knowing your rights, there are many UK laws and policies covering equality and non-discrimination in relation to sexual orientation as well.

I want a world that sees disabled people as sexual and valid prospective partners.

Mik Scarlet, a writer on sexuality and disability

The Equality and Human Rights Commission website provides information about discrimination on the grounds of disability/health and being gay or bisexual.

- Ⓦ www.equalityhumanrights.com/your-rights/equal-rights/sexual-orientation

Many people with a disability can tell you of a time when they sought to express themselves sexually, only to be thwarted by those around them. It happened to me.
Fran Vicary

If you experience a general prohibition on expressing your sexuality linked to living in residential care or using health or social care support services, you may have grounds for a formal complaint. The chapter on health and social care gives details about how to complain.

Laurence Clark, a comedian with cerebral palsy says many disabled people are in emotionally and sexually fulfilling relationships. Before getting married, he says he had mixed experiences of dating. "I found the traditional ways that people find partners, such as going to clubs and bars, didn't really work for me, as attraction in those sorts of environments is very much based on looks. But like lots of people, I tended to date through people that I met at work and people in my social networks." He says the media greatly affects disabled people's self-confidence, rarely portraying them in relationships or even as having sexual partners.

Health services are obliged by law to treat a same sex partner as next of kin, in just the same way as an opposite sex partner.

Becoming a parent

Becoming a parent for the first time is an exciting and pivotal moment in your life. Starting a family brings with it many new joys and experiences, as well as responsibilities and challenges.

If you have a disability and you are a parent, or are about to become one, you may face additional challenges when it comes to some aspects of parenthood. You are entitled to the support you need to be a 'good enough' parent.

Contacting your local social care team or family information service once you become pregnant can help you begin to plan for the future. You may be entitled to a personal budget from social services which you could use to make sure you get the support you need as someone with a disability or health condition to fulfil your parenting role. For more information see the chapter on health and social care.

The NHS provides useful information on health during pregnancy in the *Health A-Z* section of the NHS choices website:
- Health during pregnancy
- Mental health and pregnancy
- Long-term health conditions and pregnancy.

Visit the NHS choices website:
- Ⓦ www.nhs.uk

Once your baby is born, you may encounter particular challenges. These can range from problems with moving around that make it hard to pick up your child or push a buggy, to difficulties with communicating due to a hearing impairment or learning disabilities that mean you need help to read letters and understand advice.

You can use the GOV.UK website to apply for a health and social care assessment.
ⓦ www.gov.uk/apply-needs-assessment-social-services

Disability Pregnancy & Parenthood International is run by disabled parents to promote better awareness and support for disabled people during pregnancy and beyond.
ⓦ www.dppi.org.uk

There are also a few national organisations offering support for disabled parents.

Contact a Family supports families that include disabled children. It offers support, information and advice to over 340,000 families each year and campaigns for families to receive a better deal.
ⓦ www.cafamily.org.uk

Deaf Parenting UK is open to all deaf adults with responsibility for children and has a range of useful resources and factsheets.
ⓦ www.deafparent.org.uk

The Disabled Parents Network provides information, advice, advocacy and support for disabled parents and their families. They are a membership organisation that operates a peer support/contact register and a helpline run by disabled parent volunteers. They also have a range of free handbooks for parents, including *New parents* and *Getting the help you need.*
ⓦ http://disabledparentsnetwork.org.uk

The Family Rights Group provides advice sheets on a range of topics including support for disabled parents, what you can expect from your local authority, how to request help, how you will be assessed and the type of support you could receive.
ⓦ www.frg.org.uk

The NHS provides useful information for parents in the *Live Well* section of their website, including *The support you might need as a parent* and *Support for parents with learning disabilities.*
ⓦ www.nhs.uk

We are in a much better place thanks to Contact a Family. If we go to them with a problem they are always happy to help and never turn us away. The staff understand what we are going through. They see the potential in our children, and in us.

FERTILITY AND GENETIC TESTING AND COUNSELLING SERVICES

Some people with health conditions or disabilities need to use fertility services, either for reasons connected to their condition or for 'unexplained infertility'. As the chapter on health and social care services makes clear, you have a right not to be discriminated against in terms of access to fertility services.

If you want to have children and your condition has a genetic or hereditary element, you may want to consider genetic counselling services before trying to become pregnant. Genetics services can help assess the likelihood of passing your condition on to the child. GPs and hospital doctors can make referrals to genetics services, often at the request of people with a genetic condition or their families.

Genetic testing usually involves having a sample of your blood or tissue taken. The sample of cells containing your DNA can be tested to find out whether you are carrying a particular mutation and may or will develop a particular genetic condition.

There are 32 NHS genetics centres in the UK. These are organised on a regional basis and include both clinical and laboratory services, which work closely together. The Genetics Alliance provides details of these centres.

Ⓦ www.geneticalliance.org.uk/services.htm

In some cases, it may be possible through IVF to conceive a child that doesn't have a particular condition.

Geneticists will be able to explain the results of any tests or examinations that you have and help you decide how to progress.

Many people will be happy whether or not their child has the same health condition or disability. Others may wish to avoid this if possible, as being a disabled parent and parenting a disabled child may mean huge challenges as well as great joy.

You may want to talk to people with similar conditions – there are a host of organisations focussed on particular hereditary/genetic conditions.

You can contact individual organisations, such as the Cystic Fibrosis Trust or the Marfan Foundation, or get in touch with the Genetic Alliance, which brings 1200 organisations together.

Ⓦ www.geneticalliance.org

Whether or not you are disabled yourself, you may have a disabled child. There are lots of organisations that provide information about different impairments and provide advice and support services on that basis. Disabled people's organisations locally may also be able to help you navigate the services that you need.

If you are interested in the ethical aspects of genetics, Professor Adrienne Asch, a blind American woman wrote widely on the subject. Visit the Gender and Justice in the Gene Age conference website.

Ⓦ www.gjga.org

ADOPTING OR FOSTERING A CHILD

You might be interested in adopting or fostering a child, because you aren't able to have a child yourself, don't want to have a child that inherits your condition or because you are aware of the difference having parents can make to children in care.

If you are interested in adopting or fostering, you should not be unfairly discriminated against because of your health or disability. The child's needs will always be considered first and what you can offer as a parent should be judged against that.

You may be able to adopt or foster a child if you're aged 21 or over (there's no upper age limit) and either:
- single
- married (same sex and opposite sex)
- in a civil partnership
- an unmarried couple (same sex and opposite sex)
- the partner of the child's parent.

There are different rules for private adoptions and adoptions of looked-after children.

Many of the children awaiting adoption or fostering have health conditions and disabilities. Your experiences could enhance the life chances of a child with these challenges and lots of support is available if you want to consider it.

For further information on adoption, contact the British Association of Adoption and Fostering.
- Ⓦ www.baaf.org.uk

Parenting differently

You'll get lots of other tips from disabled parents if your health condition or disability means that you have to parent in a different way.

This tool from the Family and Childcare Trust can help you find local services.
- Ⓦ http://findyourfis. familyandchildcaretrust.org/kb5/ findyourfis/home.page

Former paralympian Baroness Grey-Thompson says: "Carys wore her little dungarees every day when she was a toddler. I don't have very good balance sitting upright, particularly on the left side, so to pick her up I had to lean over and lift her by the straps of her dungarees.

She learnt quickly – if she wanted a cuddle, she'd come to the right side of my chair. But if she was naughty she'd lie down flat on the left side of me where I couldn't reach her. Sometimes she'd hide under the dining table and I'd have to get out of my chair and crawl under there. At one point I resorted to a retractable dog lead to ensure some parental control. Now she's nine, and a delight."

Laurence Clark and Adele Hoskison-Clark, who both have cerebral palsy, featured in the BBC documentary *We Won't Drop the Baby,* as they prepared for the birth of their second child. They showed a positive image of disabled parents coping in their own ingenious ways with bringing up children.

Ⓦ www.bbc.co.uk/programmes/b01dwgnn

WHAT IF YOU HAVE A MENTAL HEALTH CONDITION?

In many mental health services there are peer support networks, recovery colleges and other forms of support from people who have 'been there'. You may want to explore parenting issues through those forums: there are many other parents living with mental health issues and you may find it good to talk with them.

You may be entitled to support through a health or social care personal budget, which you could use to put in place the support you need as a parent.

You may need to assert your rights, directly or with advocacy. If you feel under extra scrutiny, or if you feel you would benefit from parenting support, contact local or national mental health organisations.

The National Survivor and User Network can put you in touch with local peer support groups.

Ⓦ www.nsun.org.uk

Or get in touch with one of the national mental health charities.

Ⓦ www.mind.org.uk
Ⓦ www.rethink.org

"When I had Tilly my mental health was bad; I split up temporarily from my husband; it was a hard time and I ended up in hospital.

There was talk of taking Tilly into care. But I knew I wanted to bring her up. That motivated me. Pete and I got back together and we showed them we could do it. He has long-term mental health difficulties as well.

But each time we met a new GP or a new social worker they took one look at our diagnoses and it triggered a new attention to 'risk' and they started asking questions about whether we were capable of raising her – even though we were struggling no more than any family with a new baby.

We did need support but there was absolutely no time that Tilly was at risk. Yet time and again we have had to prove we are better parents than anyone else. Tilly is 12 now, she's happy and doing brilliantly at school – I'm really proud of her. But we had to assert our rights to achieve it."

WHAT IF YOU HAVE LEARNING DISABILITIES?

People with learning disabilities have the right to be supported in their parenting role, and their children have the right to live in a safe and supportive environment.

Unfortunately, many parents with learning disabilities don't receive the type of support they need to improve the lives of their children and keep families together.

The chance to become a parent is a basic human right. This applies equally to anyone with a learning disability but around 40% of parents with a learning disability do not have their children living with them.

Positive practice

Jack's community nurse explained what helped her to support him:

- believing that, with support, Jack would be able to adequately care for his daughter
- following the *Good practice guidance on working with parents with a learning disability* (Department of Health and Department for Education and Skills, 2007)
- supporting other professionals with how to communicate with a parent with a learning disability
- listening and hearing what Jack had to say
- ensuring that he understood all written information
- not judging
- working in partnership with everyone involved.

Jack's story

Jack has learning disabilities and is the parent of two children.

"My son, who is 12, lives with his mother, my ex-wife, but he has regular visits from me. We go to football practice and my son often has overnight stays.

From another relationship I have a daughter, Sarah, who was removed from her mother after birth. Social services assessed her mother and decided that Sarah should be adopted. I do not work any more and live in an upstairs flat. I struggled with money and had some debts. I had to ask to be assessed to care for my daughter.

At first, Sarah's mother and me had supervised contact together. Then I got a solicitor, who suggested I had another assessment from an independent social worker. This assessment was good and said that 'a plan should be considered to allow my daughter to grow up in her family of origin'. I felt that things were moving forward.

My relationship with Sarah's mother ended, and it was agreed that I could have contact with Sarah on my own, for 20 hours a week, supervised. I had lots of assessments by different people. My community nurse (learning disabilities) helped the social worker to do an assessment that was specifically for parents with a learning disability.

Finally it was decided that I could have my daughter for 47 hours a week, without supervision. Sometimes social workers would come to my house unannounced to make sure everything was okay.

Then, when Sarah was 16 months old, it was decided that she could live with me. On the day before she came home to me, I was told that court would have to decide before she could come home. I felt bad, so I telephoned my community nurse, who helped me to speak to my solicitor and my daughter's social worker, and her manager, and then they decided Sarah could come home as planned. There will be more meetings and court hearings before it is definitely decided that she can stay with me.

Having Sarah at home with me has improved my life. I feel lots of self-satisfaction because I have done everything – all the steps I had to take to satisfy the social workers. Sometimes, I can't see the point of having to do those steps, because I already have a son.

My family have helped me to get the flat decorated and they keep me right.

I thought my community nurse was the first worker who tried to help me. All the other workers would contact her and she always told me what had been said. She would read letters and reports to me because I cannot read or write very well.

She helped me to realise that it was other people's problem to give me information that I would understand, and not my problem for not being able to understand. She reminded me of appointments and times. She helped me with any problems I had with social workers, and she helped me to make telephone calls.

She came to my solicitor's with me and to court and explained things to me and for me. I did some assertiveness work with my community nurse that made me plan my life in a different way, and to think differently. I was honest with workers. I understood that my community nurse was there for me and the social worker was there for my daughter.

I had two different social workers and thought that they were honest with me about what they expected, and they would tell me if I did anything wrong. My solicitor was good at explaining things to me, and she would always write letters to my community nurse as well as me, to make sure I understood what was happening. The health visitor did not know I could not read and write very well, but when she found out she gave me information that I could understand.

My daughter is nearly two years old now, and the recommendation for the final court hearing is that my daughter remains in my care. Me and my son feel dead chuffed, and my ex-wife feels proud of me for what I did."

Change campaigns on behalf of parents with learning disabilities, for better support to keep families together. Their website lists numerous paid for and free visual and Easy Read resources on pregnancy, maternity services, having a baby, being a parent and your rights as a parent.
ⓦ www.changepeople.org/areas-of-work/parenting

Bristol University has created the Working Together with Parents Network to support parents with learning disabilities.
ⓦ www.bristol.ac.uk/wtwpn

VoiceAbility offers a range of resources for parents with learning disabilities including a picture based booklet on parenthood and an Easy Read translation service for documents.
ⓦ www.voicability.org

The British Institute of Learning Disabilities provides a range of resource material for parents with a learning disability.
ⓦ www.bild.org.uk

Best Beginnings is a small charity that provides advice and resources for parents with a learning disability.
ⓦ www.bestbeginnings.org.uk

Taking charge when people challenge your right to parent

It's possible that you will encounter negative attitudes about your right or ability to parent. This can vary from unpleasant comments in the supermarket to professionals questioning whether your child should be taken into care.

If someone is suggesting your child should be taken into care, get advice: it may be that with the right support this is not necessary.

Social services should not propose this without first finding out what support you might need as a parent living with a disability or health condition.

> The Social Care Institute for Excellence states that 'needs arising from impairment/illness and/or disabling barriers should be addressed before making judgements about parenting capacity'.

If you need advice on this, the Disabled Parents' Network has useful resources – or seek legal advice. Your local disabled people's organisation or Citizens' Advice Bureau are good places to start.

If your child is received into care because of a care order, your council will share responsibility for making most of the important decisions about your child's upbringing, including:
• who looks after them
• where they live
• how they are educated.

If you agree to your child becoming 'looked after' and there is no care order, you'll continue to have parental responsibility for your child. In either case, the council is responsible for:

- making sure that an appropriate standard of care is provided
- making sure only suitable people are employed to look after your child
- providing proper training and support to staff and foster carers
- listening to your child's views and your views about care arrangements and taking their religion, race, culture and background into account
- making sure your child has someone independent to talk to and knows how to complain if necessary.

The child may be placed with either:
- another relative
- a foster carer
- a children's home.

Care orders

Under the Children Act 1989 a council can apply to a court for a care order if it believes a child (aged under 18) is suffering or at risk of suffering significant harm.

If the court agrees, a care order allows the council to take the child into care.

Care orders last until:
- the child's 18th birthday
- an order is made giving parental responsibility to another person – eg through adoption
- the court lifts the order (this is called 'discharging' the order).

Parenting differently

Louise Milicevic and her husband both have Cerebral Palsy: "Another disabled parent helped me put things into perspective and gave me some renewed belief in my ability. She taught me techniques to lift, change, carry and feed the baby. A physiotherapist in the maternity hospital also helped us find suitable ways to handle the baby.

Since my daughter's birth I have been contacted by other expectant disabled parents facing the same negative attitudes by healthcare professionals. Based on my experience there appears to be an automatic assumption that a disabled couple will not be capable of looking after and adequately parenting a child.

Being a parent is not an easy task and dealing with physical and attitudinal barriers can make it even harder. However, it's a decision I don't regret and believe that the right to have a family should be enjoyed by everyone including disabled people, with access to appropriate support and services.

In my view the provision of a personal assistant and the whole philosophy of independent living is about giving people with disabilities the power to make choices in their own lives and should they need support to fulfil their role as parents this should be allowed as part of the service."

MAKING A COMPLAINT

If your child is in care and you're unhappy about this or how they are being treated, you can make a complaint. Talk to your child's carer or social worker first and if you're not happy, you can complain to your council.

Ⓦ www.gov.uk/complain-about-your-council

If you want your child to live with you again, seek advice from the Disabled Parent's Network or a lawyer.

Support for parents
The Family Rights Group Advice Service helpline provides confidential support for parents:
Ⓣ 0808 731 1696
Monday to Friday, 9:30am to 3:00pm

Active grandparenting and support in other relationships

Many grandparents take an active role in their grandchildren's lives. The same can be true of uncles or aunts.

If you look after your grandchildren a day a week when your son or daughter is working, or more often, or are involved in providing support to another family member or a friend, remember that the Care Act provides that your care package should take account of the things you want to do with your life. That might be socialising or undertaking adult education – or it might mean fulfilling a role within the family.

The chapter on health and social care has further details on independent living, and social care support.

Pressures on family life

The challenges that people experiencing disabilities and health conditions face can put enormous pressure on relationships. This isn't just from the fact of having a disability or health condition. It is at least as likely to result from problems with services, poverty, discrimination or harassment, in addition to the many other personal stresses that anyone can face.

There aren't statistics for different types of family pressure – between parents and children, between siblings, etc. What we do know is that families with one or more disabled children have higher than average divorce rates. For children with autism, some researchers report divorce rates of 85%.

If you feel that you personally are under pressure or someone you care about is, particularly if this is having an impact on relationships, try to take action early. Seek support from friends, family or from a disabled people's organisation where you can talk to others who understand the challenges of disability or health conditions. Or go to your GP if you believe you may be depressed, or try a counselling or relationship service if you feel a relationship is in trouble.

If you have children, and are worried about the impact on them of raising concerns about your health and wellbeing, seek the support of a formal or informal advocate. This could be a friend or a professional who can represent you and accompany you to any meetings with health, social care or other professionals.

Some local councils have their own advocacy services. To find out if there are any in your area, contact your local council or check its website. To find your council's contact details:
- ⓦ www.gov.uk/find-your-local-council

If you have a care coordinator from your local social services or healthcare team, they should be able to liaise with other agencies with or for you.

Diabetes UK offers an advocacy service for people with diabetes that is available in many areas of England and Wales.
- ⓔ advocacy@diabetes.org.uk
- ⓦ www.diabetes.org.uk

Age UK gives advice and information to older people and their carers, family, friends and other people involved in their care. Some branches offer advocacy services. Find your local branch on their website.
- ⓣ 0800 169 6565
- ⓦ www.ageuk.org.uk

Carers UK has a free advice line for carers. Visit their website for advice on many aspects of caring. Carers UK doesn't provide an advocacy service, but can give you information on where to go for help.
- ⓣ 0808 808 7777
- ⓦ www.carersuk.org

Relate provides counselling, support and information for all relationships – for couples and for families. You can locate counselling services near you via their website.
- ⓣ 0300 100 1234
- ⓦ www.relate.org.uk

Domestic violence

If you are experiencing domestic violence, or think that someone you know or care for might be, seek help straightaway. Many people feel trapped but there will be a solution.

The National Centre for Domestic Violence (NCDV) provides a free, fast emergency injunction service to survivors of domestic violence regardless of their financial circumstances, race, gender or sexual orientation.

The service allows anyone to apply for an injunction within 24 hours of first contact (in most circumstances).

The Centre works in close partnership with the police, local firms of solicitors and other support agencies (Refuge, Women's Aid etc) to help survivors obtain speedy protection.
- ⓣ 0844 8044 999
  (Choose option 1 for information about getting an injunction)
  Textphone 0800 9702070
  Text NCDV to 60777
- ⓦ www.ncdv.org.uk

National helpline

The 24-Hour National Domestic Violence Helpline, run in partnership between Women's Aid and Refuge, is a national service for women experiencing domestic violence, their family, friends, colleagues and others calling on their behalf.
- ⓣ 0808 2000 247 (freephone)
- ⓦ www.nationaldomestic violencehelpline.org.uk

Sometimes, partner relationships break down. Family mediators are trained to help separating couples reach money, property and childcare agreements without going to court.

Clients may qualify for legal aid to help with mediation costs should a dispute arise from a family relationship.
Ⓦ www.gov.uk/legal-aid-family-mediation

If you are married or in a civil partnership and your relationship ends, you should get advice before embarking on a formal separation, end to a civil partnership or divorce to ensure a settlement that takes account of disability and is fair to everyone.
Ⓦ www.gov.uk/divorce

The Sexuality and disability website has lots of useful information about sex, relationships and parenthood.
Ⓦ www.sexualityanddisability.org.uk

Family life and social care support

You or your partner or child may need social care support. The chapter on health and social care services gives details.

If you or someone you live with needs social care support, you should not need to be separated. The right to family life means you should be able to get care at home, or, perhaps particularly if you and your partner are both older, to move together into a residential or nursing home.

Children supporting adults

More than 155,000 children in the UK support a family member as a result of disability, health condition or other challenging situation such as drugs or alcohol. This number is rising.

A child might be doing things like the following on a regular basis because an adult is unable to, and other support is not available:
- cooking
- cleaning
- shopping
- providing nursing and personal care
- giving emotional support.

If your child is supporting you, do make sure that you have claimed any support that you may be entitled to – either in social security benefits such as Disability Living Allowance or Personal Independence Payment, which can help with mobility and help at home, or through payments or services from your local authority.

Parents with disabilities and health conditions should not have to rely on our children for help, as we have statutory rights to 'practical assistance in the home' and to the adaptations and equipment we require.

However, tight eligibility criteria may mean that, even once you have claimed whatever you are entitled to, your child may have to do more for you or at home than is usual because of your health condition or disability.

If so, it's important that they get the opportunity to learn and to play; to complete their education satisfactorily and get enough support and rest themselves. Being able to talk to other young people supporting disabled or older people can make a huge difference.

It's also important that you get the support you need as a parent. If, for instance, you get an interpreter when you see a health professional, then there is no need for your child to interpret – and it is not appropriate for a child to be the interpreter. If you have support for cooking and cleaning, it can relieve the child and mean you are clearly in the parenting role.

The Children's Society runs the Include Programme, which works with young carers and helps voluntary and statutory services to support young carers.
Ⓦ www.childrenssociety.org.uk
Ⓦ www.youngcarer.com

Barnardo's runs services across the UK which work to support young carers and their families in a variety of ways.
Ⓦ www.barnardos.org.uk

Children supporting adults can find helpful information in the *Being a young carer* section of the NHS choices website.
Ⓦ www.nhs.uk

Set up by Carers Trust, YCNet is an online support service for people in the UK aged 18 and under, who help to look after someone in their family with an illness, disability, drug or alcohol addiction or mental health condition.
Ⓦ www.youngcarers.net

Seventeen-year-old Rebecca from Flintshire has been using the Barnardo's Cymru Flintshire young carers service for six years. She helped her mother care for her disabled father and take care of her younger sister.

"I used to have to help mum with getting things for dad and making sure he was comfortable. A lot of the time I would have to look after my sister when mum was busy caring for my dad."

Rebecca used to miss out on seeing friends and going out because she was so busy helping her mum look after her dad and sister. "You don't really realise you're missing out on anything because it's just what you're used to. But I started to realise I was different a few years before my dad passed away when my friends were developing their social lives".

Barnardo's Cymru Flintshire young carers service helped her to enjoy her childhood through taking part in many different activities and events.

"That's one of the great things about the project, we get to go to all these different places and do so many different activities which I've never done before and wouldn't have had the chance to do without them. That's why the young carers project is so great, it helps young carers develop another life other than the one they have at home."

Your rights

If you experience a change in your life or circumstances, your rights are protected by a number of laws and international treaties to ensure you are treated with fairness, equality, dignity, respect and autonomy.

This is true of your right to family life. Under the United Nations Convention on the Rights of People with Disabilities (UNCRPD) the family is considered central to the way we live.

Ⓦ www.un.org/disabilities/convention/conventionfull.shtml

Article 22 explains someone with a disability or health condition is entitled to maintain their privacy, their family, and their home life without interference.

Article 28 sets out the right to an adequate standard of living for you and your family.

The Human Rights Act 1998 also means that people with disabilities and health conditions have a right to have their 'private life' and 'family life' respected by the state in the UK. Visit the British Institute of Human Rights for more information.

Ⓦ www.bihr.org.uk

THE RIGHTS OF PARENTS

The right to have children is a basic human right and the UNCRPD sets out your right to become a parent and the rights of your children.

Article 23 outlines your right to marry, to start a family, and to bring up your children.

The Equality Act 2010 protects parents with disabilities and health conditions from discrimination. Parenting classes, for example, should make 'reasonable adjustments' to make them accessible.

You should not be denied fertility treatment, and you must be treated fairly by adoption or fostering services.

Information should also be accessible – so for instance a hospital should provide forms in Braille or large print to assist you if you're blind or have a visual impairment.

THE RIGHTS OF CHILDREN

International treaties and UK law also protect your children's rights.

Article 23 of the UNCRPD explains that the child's best interests must always come first and it is the state's responsibility to give appropriate support to enable anyone with a disability to carry out their role as a parent.

THE RIGHTS OF OLDER PEOPLE

You may have read about poor treatment of older people in their own homes or in residential care. You may even have personal experience of this.

It is vital that you have access to information about your human rights so you can challenge poor treatment and demand better services. This is particularly true for older people and the Human Rights Act includes specific protections for older people.

Perhaps most importantly, these include:
- the right not to be tortured or treated in an inhuman or degrading way
- the right to respect for private and family life, home and correspondence
- the right to life.

Older people, and the organisations and individuals that support them, are increasingly using the Human Rights Act to challenge poor treatment and improve public services.

There is currently no specific treaty for older people, although the United Nations has produced the *UN Principles for Older Persons* (1991). While this is not legally binding, it is an important statement of the human rights that should be universally afforded to older people. For more information visit:
- ⓦ www.equalrightstrust.org

The British Institute of Human Rights has published a useful guide to human rights for older people.
- ⓦ www.bihr.org.uk

Age UK provides a wide range of information on your rights as an older person.
- ⓦ www.ageuk.org.uk/professional-resources-home/services-and-practice/equalities-and-human-rights

You don't lose your right to participate in family life just because you are older – and it doesn't just relate to parents and children. If you have grandchildren and need support, this should include supporting regular contact with them.

How to complain

If you have a complaint about the NHS or a local authority, you'll find details of how to complain in the health and social care chapter.

It's a good idea to keep a written record of what has happened to you and when, as well as to whom you've spoken, what action you've taken and any response you receive.

The Equality and Human Rights Commission has advice on considering which complaints process to follow.
- ⓦ www.equalityhumanrights.com/your-rights/equal-rights/using-your-rights/deciding-whether-to-make-a-claim

The Equality Advisory Support Service and the Citizens Advice Bureau can advise you on how to pursue a complaint about discrimination.
- ⓦ www.equalityadvisoryservice.com
- ⓦ www.adviceguide.org.uk/england/about_this_site/get_advice.htm

The Law Centres Network set up across parts of the UK can provide you with impartial legal advice.
- ⓦ www.lawcentres.org.uk

Disability Rights UK has additional advice on your rights and how to make a complaint in this factsheet.
- ⓦ www.disabilityrightsuk.org/making-complaint

Benefits and tax credits – everything you need to know?

If your life is affected by disability, welfare reform and changes to social security have made getting the support you need even more of a challenge. Keeping up with the ever-changing rules is crucial.

Trusted by claimants and advisers for over 40 years

The Handbook provides in-depth information on the entire benefits system. Written in plain English, our user-friendly benefits guide is designed for both claimants and advisers. Updated every year, it has the answers you need to provide advice or claim what you're entitled to.

As comprehensive as ever

- Benefits for people of all ages with an illness, injury or disability
- Benefits for carers, people looking for work or in retirement
- Personal Independence Payment: help with care or getting around
- Universal Credit: Who is eligible and how it's worked out
- Challenging benefit decisions; how to appeal
- Tools and tactics to help you make a successful claim

Published May each year

You can buy our publications online at www.disabilityrightsuk.org

Money

If you've recently developed a long-term health condition or disability – or it has changed – then the last thing on your mind may be your finances. However, it makes sense to try and sort out your money situation as soon as you can.

Money matters to all of us. Making sure you stay out of or manage and reduce debt, earn as much as you need or claim any social security benefits you are entitled to, are all part of it. But so is thinking through your current and future needs, planning and budgeting and getting value for money from any disability-related expenditure.

Staying in work

If you are working and develop a disability or health condition, or your condition worsens, try to stay with your employer if you can. You may need some time off to adjust to your new situation – that doesn't mean you have to leave your job altogether. It's usually much easier going back to a job and a workplace that you know after a period of leave than starting somewhere new.

In most cases, work is good for our health. While employers are becoming more enlightened, your chances of being in work will probably be greatest if you stay in contact with people who know you.

Your rights

You have rights that can help you keep your job, even if you need time off for medical treatment or adjusting to a new condition.

To find out about employee rights to paid sick leave and employer's duties to make reasonable adjustments:

Ⓦ www.gov.uk/taking-sick-leave

Working flexibly

"I've got arthritis. It's up and down. A fluctuating condition, as the doctors say. I can't plan for flare-ups but I can plan my working life for joint replacement surgery and early retirement. I try to earn as much as I can while I'm well because I know that in the future I won't be able to work so hard. My philosophy is work hard while you can. I put a bit of money away each month – a regular amount plus, if I've had a good month, a little bit extra. This approach meant that when I needed to take a break from full-time work for a while, I was able to. For me, saving is a key part of managing a long-term health condition."

You can apply for Access to Work (see the chapter on learning and working) to provide support in the form of equipment, help with travel costs or a personal assistant. Make sure your employer knows about this when you are talking about coming back to or staying in work.

If your current job no longer works for you and you've explored different options with your employer, seek help getting a new job, for example from Jobcentre Plus.

You might also consider self-employment. There are advantages and disadvantages to running a business or working for yourself when you are disabled or have a long-term health condition.

Being my own boss
"When one of my twins was born with a disability I had to stop work. It put a lot of pressure on my husband and on the family finances. Then eBay came along. I sold the clothes and toys they'd grown out of. Then I sold all the old toys from my childhood. I was surprised how easy it was and how much I made on them. So I started buying toys from the 60s and 70s at car-boot sales and in charity shops and selling them on eBay.

Before I knew it I was running my own small business from home. It's fun, brings in the money and I still have all the time I need with my daughters."

You can manage the work yourself, when, where and how it suits you – and work when you are well and take time out when you are not. But there is no guarantee of an earned income and this can be hard to manage.

Look for support if you are considering self-employment. Disability Means Business is a website for disabled entrepreneurs who are self-employed or wishing to start up their own business.
Ⓦ www.disabilitymeansbusiness.com

Turn2us is a free service that helps people in financial need to access welfare benefits, charitable grants and other financial help – online, by phone and face to face through its partner organisations. They also provide information on self-employment.
Ⓣ 0808 802 2000
Ⓦ www.turn2us.org.uk

Working Tax Credit
If you are in work and struggling to manage financially, you may be able to claim Working Tax Credit to top up your wages. You must normally be working for a least 30 hours a week to be eligible (although this can be reduced to 16 hours a week in some circumstances).

To claim, call the Tax Credit Helpline:
Ⓣ 0345 300 3900

If you lose your job
If you're employed – but unable to work – you may be able to get Statutory Sick Pay (SSP) from your employer for up to 28 weeks. Some employers have more generous sick pay schemes, so check with your employer.

If you haven't been able to work for more than 28 weeks because of a health condition or disability, you may be able to get Employment and Support Allowance.

EMPLOYMENT AND SUPPORT ALLOWANCE

Employment and Support Allowance (ESA) has two elements: income-related ESA, which is dependent upon your income – and contributory ESA, which is dependent on your National Insurance contribution record. Contributory ESA is often paid for a limited period of 12 months. You may receive one or both of these elements, depending on your circumstances.

Income-related ESA is slowly being replaced by Universal Credit.

The Work Capability Assessment
Your entitlement to ESA, the level it is paid and whether it is time-limited or not (in the case of contributory ESA) is determined by a points-based test called a 'Work Capability Assessment'.

You will first need to complete a form: the 'Limited capability for work questionnaire'. Make sure you know how the points are worked out when you are completing this form.

If you are unhappy with the result of the Work Capability Assessment, it is worth asking the DWP to look at the decision again, and appealing to a tribunal if they do not change the decision. Tribunals are independent, and many such decisions are overturned at tribunal.

If you are not entitled to ESA, you may be able to claim Jobseeker's Allowance.

For more information on ESA, see Disability Rights UK's factsheet:
- Ⓦ www.disabilityrightsuk.org/ employment-and-support-allowance-overview

JOBSEEKER'S ALLOWANCE

Jobseeker's Allowance (JSA) has two elements; income-based JSA, which is dependant on your income – and contribution-based JSA, which is dependant on your National Insurance contribution record. Contribution-based JSA is paid for a limited period of six months.

To be eligible for JSA, you need to be available for and actively seeking work.

Income-based JSA is slowly being replaced by Universal Credit.

You can claim JSA by phone or online:
- Ⓣ 0800 055 6688
- Ⓦ www.gov.uk/jobseekers-allowance/ how-to-claim

Find out more about Statutory Sick Pay, Employment Support Allowance and Jobseeker's Allowance from Disability Rights UK's *Disability Rights Handbook*.
- Ⓦ www.disabilityrightsuk.org

INSURANCE POLICIES

You should also check whether you have insurance policies that would cover your mortgage payments or replace a percentage of your income.

For example:
- income protection insurance
- short-term income protection insurance
- payment protection insurance
- mortgage payment protection insurance
- critical illness insurance.

Claim straight away – there's usually a waiting period before the policy pays out, so the sooner you send your claim, the better.

Reviewing the situation

If you have a health condition or disability, you may be off work for a while and your costs may change. Review your budget and make sure you're not spending more than you have coming in and think through how to make the most of the money you have.

If you need money immediately, you could be entitled to benefits that will:
- help you manage the extra costs associated with being disabled or having a long-term health condition (for example, Personal Independence Payment or Attendance Allowance)
- replace earnings if you lose your job (for example, Employment and Support Allowance)
- top-up your income (for example, Tax Credits or Pension Credit)
- help you with essential costs (for example, Housing Benefit).

The Government's benefits calculator can help you work out what your income would be if you claim all that you are entitled to:
- Ⓦ www.gov.uk/benefits-calculators

MAKE A PLAN

The Money Advice Website has a useful budget planner to find out how you could adjust to your new financial circumstances:
- Ⓦ www.moneyadviceservice.org.uk/en/tools/budget-planner

Published annually, the *Disability Rights Handbook* is a comprehensive guide to benefits for people with disabilities and health conditions that could help you maximise your income. If you want the full picture on benefits, our handbook contains all the detail.
- Ⓣ 020 7250 8191
- Ⓦ www.disabilityrightsuk.org

CONTACT YOUR ENERGY SUPPLIERS

Get in touch with your gas and electricity suppliers as soon as possible. Tell them that you have a long-term health condition or a disability. Ask them:
- whether you are paying the lowest possible price
- to register you for their priority service – this provides some services free of charge such as annual safety checks and emergency call-out priority
- about extra protection from disconnection – to prevent you from being cut off
- whether they provide free insulation, which can reduce your heating costs.

Find out more about help with utility bills on the NHS Choices website:
- Ⓦ www.nhs.uk/CarersDirect/moneyandlegal/finance/Pages/Utilitybills.aspx

CHECK YOUR WORKPLACE PENSION

If you've been paying into a workplace pension, ask your employer or the company that runs the scheme whether there are any ill-health benefits you might be entitled to. If there are, find out how much they're worth and how long they will last.

FIND OUT IF YOU CAN GET SUPPORT SERVICES

If your condition means you have difficulty getting around or doing day-to-day tasks, your council (in England, Scotland and Wales) or health and social care board (in Northern Ireland) might provide support with things like:

- small adaptations to your home (like handrails on your bath)
- special equipment related to your health condition or impairment
- shopping and cleaning
- personal care and day-to-day tasks.

The chapter on health and social care gives further details.

SEE IF YOU QUALIFY FOR HELP WITH HEALTH COSTS

NHS prescriptions are free in Northern Ireland, Scotland and Wales. If you live in England, prescriptions are free if you're on certain means-tested benefits (such as income-related Employment and Support Allowance) or if you are over 60. People with certain medical conditions – including diabetes and cancer – get a medical exemption certificate which means they don't have to pay for prescriptions.

If you're not sure whether your condition qualifies, check with your GP or consultant or go to:

- Ⓦ www.nhs.uk/NHSEngland/ Healthcosts/Pages/Prescriptioncosts. aspx

Taking charge

Prescriptions

You may be able to save money on prescriptions in England by buying a 'prepayment certificate', which covers you for all the prescriptions you need for a set period. This is often cheaper than paying for prescriptions one at a time.

To find out more:
- Ⓣ 0300 330 1341
- Ⓦ www.nhs.uk/nhsengland/ healthcosts/pages/ppc.aspx

You may be able to apply for free prescriptions (and help towards other NHS charges or the cost of travel to and from hospital appointments) through the NHS Low Income scheme.
- Ⓣ 0300 330 1343
- Ⓦ www.nhs.uk/NHSEngland/ Healthcosts/Pages/nhs-low-income-scheme.aspx

Make your money easier to manage by yourself

You can make it easier to manage your money when you're not well by either simplifying your arrangements or getting help from someone you know and trust. You might even like to do both these things. This can really help if you suddenly have less time or energy, for example because you are attending lots of medical appointments.

Follow these five steps to simpler money management.

Step 1 – get paid straight into your bank account

It's normally easier to have your income paid straight into your bank account – you can still do this if you're on benefits, getting sick pay or working part-time. Getting paid like this is great because:

- it saves you trips to the bank
- you don't have to wait for a cheque to clear before getting your money
- it's safer than carrying cash around with you.

If you haven't got a bank account and think you might have trouble opening one because you have a low income or a poor credit history, for example, you could apply for a basic bank account – these are the easiest to get.

Step 2 – use direct debits and standing orders for bills

Once you've done your budget and know you've got enough coming in to match your spending, switch your regular bills to direct debit or standing order. This will help because:

- you won't need to worry about getting to the bank or the postbox
- payments will be taken automatically so you won't face any late payment penalties
- many companies, councils and organisations give a discount for people paying by direct debit.

But be careful if your budget isn't balanced – bounced direct debits and standing orders can leave you facing heavy bank charges.

Step 3 – make online payments or use telephone banking

For bills you can't pay by direct debit or standing order, see if you can pay them using online or telephone banking services.

Taking charge of your money

"I keep a little over £1000 in my current account, which is the minimum to avoid bank charges, and every month I transfer all the excess to a higher interest saving account.

It takes about five minutes to do this online and I usually earn a couple of quid a month in interest. This doesn't translate into a bad hourly rate and it all adds up during the year.

Because I'm not able to go out as often as I'd like, I spend a lot of time on the telephone. I discovered that I could use a programme to make telephone calls from my computer. It's free to other users and at a far cheaper rate than usual to all other numbers.

Now I'm not counting the minutes when I'm on the phone. I went on a computer course at my local library and now I realise how much you can do – I'm about to download an app on my smartphone so I can also get free calls from there.

I rent DVDs online now and then there's free music, free radio, free TV programmes. If you use the right software and go to the right sites, it's legal."

Step 4 – use online or phone banking to keep track of your balances

It's important to keep a close eye on your bank balance so you don't go overdrawn and have to pay extra charges. Online or phone banking can keep you up-to-date easily if you're at home. If you see some trouble ahead, think about calling your bank before they have to call you.

Step 5 – get support from your bank

Banks have to make their information and services as accessible as possible for customers with disabilities and health conditions. Support you can request includes:

- bank statements and other documents in Braille, large print and audio formats
- ATMs (cashpoint machines) that are wheelchair accessible and have text-to-speech functionality (so-called 'talking ATMs' which safeguard your security through headphones)
- chip and signature cards for those customers who are unable to memorise a PIN
- low-level counters in branch and counters fitted with a hearing induction loop.

Ask your bank what support they can offer you.

Getting someone else to help you with your money

If you need help to do certain things, like deciding how much money to spend on what or getting cash out of the bank, you can get help and support from a friend or family member. Lots of people do this and it can be a weight off your mind.

Talk it over

"I got screwed by credit cards. At one time I must have had a dozen. I sensed things were getting out of control but I thought, 'Well, it can't be that bad if they keep giving me new cards'. It was. It was worse. I was able to bounce along the bottom for a bit by just paying the minimum payments but then the mortgage rate went up a bit and we had a pay freeze at work – both little things in themselves but they were enough. Suddenly I couldn't meet all my minimum payments. The trouble is that debt is a psychological thing – it stresses you out and you want to spend to relieve the stress. You're wearing all these nice clothes and you kid yourself you're OK. It's like believing your own publicity. I was terrified to talk to my girlfriend about my problems. I was insecure and my spending was part of that. I think I thought she was only interested in me because I was cool and carefree but it brought us closer in fact.

I'm not recommending debt as a way to improve your relationship but I am recommending being as honest as you can."

Any person you choose to act for you should be someone you can trust completely and you should check that they're happy to do it.

> **Get advice and support**
>
> "When I had my first bad bout of depression even I didn't realise. Financially, two things happened: after a period of manic spending, I lost my job. In hindsight I suppose I thought I could spend my way to happiness. Put the two together and soon I was in big trouble. If I didn't realise I was depressed, you can bet that the bank didn't. It's taken me a long time to get back on my feet.
>
> "At first I didn't want to claim benefits, but a money advisor pointed out that I'd paid in well over £100,000 in tax and national insurance in the years I'd been working. That focused the mind and I was happy to claim for a while until I got back into work. Benefits are fine but work gives you control.
>
> "I've now got a diagnosis for my bi-polar disorder, which the bank knows about, so I'm hoping they'll be more understanding if this happens again. But with a bit of luck, it won't even if I'm ill again. Why? Because now I'm aware of the problem, I've started to think about my finances consciously. I'd never done that before. It's not difficult. And knowing how much I've got coming in and going out each month puts me in control, which reduces my stress levels and so reduces the chances of me slipping into a depression again."

When you know who you want to help you, you can decide what help you need. There are different options to choose from, depending on your circumstances.

> **Taking charge**
>
> **Your money**
> - Do you have difficulty with some money tasks but not others?
> - Do you go through periods when you find it hard to manage, but can cope at other times?
> - Work out what suits you and your situation best.

HELP WITH BANK ACCOUNTS

Third-party mandates

A third-party mandate is a document that tells your bank, building society or other account provider that they can accept instructions about your money from someone else – a named person. It gives that person the authority to run your bank account (but no other financial arrangements) for you.

The account and the money in it are still yours, but the person helping you can make withdrawals and arrange other transactions like paying bills. They can do all the things to run the account that you can.

Contact your bank or other account provider to request a third-party mandate arrangement.

Joint accounts

You can open a joint account with someone else, or change an account you already have so that it is held in joint names. In this case, the money in the account no longer belongs just to you.

You and the other person become joint owners.

With a joint account, you can both withdraw money and take other decisions without asking each other. If you set up a joint account so that someone can help you pay bills and other expenses, think about keeping a separate personal account for money that isn't used for bills.

If either of you dies, the other person automatically inherits all the money in the account and is able to spend it. If one of you runs up debts on the account, the other would be liable for the debts too. So you need to be sure that you're opening a joint account with someone you trust completely.

To set up a joint account, contact your bank or other account provider.

Set up a Post Office® card account
If your benefits are paid into this type of account and you find it hard to get to a post office yourself, you can ask for a named person (called your 'permanent agent') to have access to your account as well. They will be given their own card and PIN so they can draw out cash and check your balance for you.

> If someone offers to help with your bank account, Post Office® card account or other account, don't just give them your own card and PIN. You will be breaking the security rules and, if money goes missing, you might not be protected.

SET UP AN ORDINARY POWER OF ATTORNEY
A power of attorney is a legal arrangement that gives someone else the power to make decisions for you.

Some powers of attorney are designed to last indefinitely. But you can set up an arrangement called an 'ordinary power of attorney'. This is designed to be used – often for a specific, short period or for a specific task – when you're able to make your own decisions but it's convenient to ask someone else to take over. An ordinary power of attorney can be useful if, for example:
* you'll be in hospital for a time
* you're able to make your own decisions but want someone else to be able to step in with support from time to time.

An ordinary power of attorney can cover all your financial affairs (a 'general power') or just some areas that you specify, like dealing with the tax office or selling a house.

You can cancel the arrangement at any time. An ordinary power of attorney is automatically invalid if you lose the ability to make your own decisions. If you want a power of attorney that will continue even if you lose the ability to make your own decisions, you will need to make a lasting power of attorney (called a continuing power of attorney in Scotland and an enduring power of attorney in Northern Ireland).

To set up an ordinary power of attorney, it may be helpful to contact a solicitor, who will make a charge for this service.

But before you spend any money, check that your bank and any other providers will recognise the power and accept your attorney's instructions.

A Citizens Advice Bureau may also be able to help.

PLANNING FOR WHEN YOU CAN'T MAKE FINANCIAL DECISIONS

If you know you're going to find it more difficult to make decisions in the future – for example, because of a progressive health condition (such as dementia) that will affect your mental capacity – you might want to set up a lasting or continuing power of attorney. This will allow someone you trust to make financial decisions for you in the long-term.

Plan ahead
You can set up a power of attorney only while you're still able to make decisions.

You can set up a legal arrangement that gives someone else the right to make decisions about your finances on your behalf. This arrangement has different names in different parts of the UK:
- in England and Wales – lasting power of attorney
- in Northern Ireland – enduring power of attorney
- in Scotland – continuing power of attorney.

Who to choose as your attorney
Most people appoint their husband, wife, partner, other family member or a close friend as their attorney. It must be someone you trust completely.

Your attorney will take decisions for you, but should always act in your best interests. Your attorney can be a company – for example, a firm of solicitors or a bank. Companies will charge a fee for providing this service.

Taking charge

Choosing an attorney
- Choose someone you trust completely.
- It's a good idea to name one or more replacement attorneys who would take over if your first choice died or couldn't act for you anymore.
- Make sure they are willing to act for you.
- Talk over your affairs with them, so that they know what's involved, what your wishes would be and where to find your paperwork, including the power of attorney document itself.
- Register the power of attorney in plenty of time.
- It takes several weeks to register and even if you have already lost mental capacity, your attorney wouldn't be able to act for you in that time. So it makes sense to plan in advance.

Making a power of attorney – your next steps
In itself, setting up the power of attorney doesn't take control away from you. It can't be used until it's been formally registered. You don't have to register it straight away – you can set up the power of attorney now and only get it registered when it's going to be needed.

Remember, your attorney has to act in your best interests after the power of attorney is set up, taking account of what you would want.

Types of lasting power of attorney

The big differences between the types of power of attorney are the decisions they cover – financial ones, or ones about your health and welfare. The options available depend on where you live.

In England and Wales there are two types of lasting power of attorney. You can set up one or both.

- A 'property and financial affairs lasting power of attorney' lets someone manage all your financial affairs – for example, running your bank and savings accounts, managing your tax affairs, and buying and selling investments and property.
- A 'health and welfare lasting power of attorney' lets someone make decisions about your health, care and welfare – for example, what medical treatment you receive and whether you move into a care home.

In Northern Ireland there is only one type of power of attorney, an 'enduring power of attorney'. It lets someone manage all your financial affairs, similar to the English property and financial affairs lasting power of attorney. There isn't a power of attorney that lets someone make decisions about your health and well-being.

In Scotland there are two types of lasting power of attorney.

- A 'continuing power of attorney' lets someone manage all your financial affairs.
- A 'welfare power of attorney' lets someone make decisions about your care and welfare.

Living within my means

"I took medical retirement from the civil service with chronic fatigue syndrome. I'd prefer to still be working and making a contribution if I could but in the end it was the best thing to do. My wife and I downsized. We got a smaller house and totally re-evaluated our expenditure. Smaller carbon footprint and all that. It's amazing how much money you waste when you're not counting the pennies. I feel good about living more simply. I understand myself better and what's important in life."

Retirement

Once you reach state pension age, you may be able to claim State Pension. If your State Pension is not enough to live on, you may be able to claim Pension Credit.

STATE PENSION AGE

State pension age is currently 65 for men; for women it is being gradually increased each year and will also be 65 by 2018. For men and women, the state pension age will be higher in the future. Contact the Pension Service or check the State Pension calculator for details:

ⓦ www.gov.uk/calculate-state-pension

STATE PENSION

How much State Pension you get depends on the National Insurance contributions that you have paid over the years. It may include an additional amount based on your earnings.

You can claim by phone or online:
- **T** 0800 731 7898
- **W** www.gov.uk/claim-state-pension-online

PENSION CREDIT

Pension Credit is a means-tested benefit. It can top up any State Pension you are getting. It can also help towards mortgage interest payments (see below). You must have reached the qualifying age to claim it; this is being raised from 60 to 66 between 2010 and 2020.

You can claim Pension Credit by phone:
- **T** 0800 991 234

Taking charge

Your money

If you know what you are entitled to it can make a big difference as you plan your finances.

Think about all the different sources of income – from any employment or self-employment, pensions, interest on savings, benefits and tax credits; and think about how to manage your spending.

With a mixture of good planning and knowing your rights you have the best chance of making your money work for you and the life you want.

Caring responsibilities

If you are not able to work full time because you have to care for someone with a disability or long-term health condition, you may be able to claim Carer's Allowance. If this is not enough to live on, you may be able to claim Income Support to top up the Carer's Allowance.

CARER'S ALLOWANCE

Carer's Allowance is a benefit for people who regularly spend at least 35 hours a week caring for a disabled person.

To be entitled, you do not need to be living with the disabled person, or be related to them, but they do need to be receiving a 'qualifying benefit'.

The daily living component of Personal Independence Payment is a qualifying benefit, as is Attendance Allowance.

You can get a claim-form for Carer's Allowance by calling:
- **T** 0845 608 4321

Or claim online at:
- **W** www.gov.uk/apply-carers-allowance

INCOME SUPPORT

Income Support is a means-tested benefit (slowly being replaced by Universal Credit). It can top up any Carer's Allowance you are getting. It can also help towards mortgage interest payments (see below).

You can claim Income Support by phone:
- **T** 0800 055 6688

Paying your mortgage

If you are struggling to meet your mortgage payments, it's worth checking that you are getting all of the benefits and tax credits you are entitled to. It can make a real difference to your income and help with expenses.

SUPPORT FOR MORTGAGE INTEREST

If you are a homeowner who is getting certain income-related benefits, you may be able to get help towards interest payments on your mortgage or on loans for repairs and improvements to your home.

This help is paid as part of your benefit and is called support for mortgage interest (SMI). SMI is normally paid direct to your lender. You can't get help towards capital repayments – only the interest.

You cannot normally get SMI until after a 'waiting period', which is 13 weeks after you first claimed benefit. If you're getting Pension Credit, there is no waiting period.

Which benefits help you get support for mortgage interest?
You must be getting one of the following benefits to qualify for SMI:
* Income Support
* Income-based Jobseeker's Allowance
* Income-related Employment and Support Allowance
* Pension Credit
* Universal Credit.

If you're getting income-based Jobseeker's Allowance, you can only get this help for a maximum of two years.

This time limit does not apply to the other benefits listed above.

Remember that rules may change and it is always worth checking online for the most up-to-date information.

To check if you can get SMI, contact Jobcentre Plus:
* 0800 055 6688 (new claims)
* www.gov.uk/contact-jobcentre-plus

Or the Pension Service:
* 0800 991 234
* http://pensions-service.direct.gov.uk/en/find-pension-centre/home.asp

If you start getting behind with your mortgage payments it's important to get advice as soon as possible. Advice is available from lenders and agencies such as Citizens Advice and Shelter. A good starting point is www.gov.uk.

Lenders are now required to consider all options before taking steps to repossess a property. These can include agreeing to reduce your mortgage payments for a set time, changing your payments to interest-only, giving you a payment holiday, or letting you stay in the property while you find somewhere else to live.

If you are unhappy about how your lender has been dealing with you, you can complain to the Financial Ombudsman:
* 0800 023 4567
* www.financial-ombudsman.org.uk

You'll find more information about help with mortgage payments in the chapter on money.

Housing Benefit

You may be eligible for Housing Benefit to help pay your rent if you are on a low income or on other social security benefits.

You can apply for it if you live in social housing or if you rent privately. Your income and savings have to be under certain limits for you to qualify.

Taking charge

Claiming what you are entitled to
Provide as much information as possible when you apply for Housing Benefit. Tell the council immediately about changes in your circumstances.

Your Housing Benefit may be restricted by the 'bedroom tax' (if you rent from a council or housing association) or the benefits cap.

If you are claiming certain other security benefits, such as Employment and Support Allowance, you can claim Housing Benefit at the same time.

Disability Rights UK publishes a range of factsheets which include:
- Housing benefit
- Help with council tax
- Housing grants
- Help with heating
- The WaterSure scheme

You can find our factsheets about the bedroom tax and the benefits cap in our website:
- Ⓦ www.disabilityrightsuk.org/how-we-can-help

Otherwise, you can ask your council for a Housing Benefit claim-form or you can download an HCTB1 from:
- Ⓦ www.gov.uk/housing-benefit/how-to-claim

Help with Council Tax

You can apply to your council to get money off your Council Tax bill if you're on a low income. This can apply whether you are in or out of work.

Several schemes can help. The 'Disability Reduction scheme' can help if you or any other resident in your home is 'substantially and permanently disabled'.

At least one of the following three conditions must also be met:
- you have an additional bathroom or kitchen needed by the disabled person
- you have a room (other than a bathroom, kitchen or toilet) needed by and predominantly used by that person
- you have enough space in your dwelling for that person to use a wheelchair indoors.

The 'Discount scheme' applies if you live alone (or can be treated as living alone). General 'Council Tax Reduction schemes' also apply.

In England and Wales each council has a different scheme. In Scotland there is a nationwide scheme. Contact your council to see what help is available in your area.

Council Tax does not apply in Northern Ireland, which has 'rates' instead:
Ⓦ www.nidirect.gov.uk/index/information-and-services/property-and-housing/rates/help-with-paying-your-rates.htm

Other benefits and advice

This chapter has explored some of the options for maximising your income through work or benefits.

You'll find further information on managing your money on the Money Advice Service website:
Ⓦ www.moneyadviceservice.org.uk

To find out more about benefits, see Disability Rights UK's *Disability Rights Handbook*.
Ⓣ 020 7250 8191
Ⓦ www.disabilityrightsuk.org

Financial support for mobility and care needs

Disability Living Allowance (DLA) and the Personal Independence Payment (PIP) provide help towards the extra costs of disability. They are not means tested and are paid on top of almost any other income you have. They can also give you access to other types of help.

DISABILITY LIVING ALLOWANCE

DLA is for children under age 16. From age 16, a young person can claim PIP instead. Before PIP was introduced in 2013, disabled adults under 65 could also claim DLA. If you still get DLA as an adult under 65, you will be re-assessed for PIP at some point. Your DLA continues as normal if you were aged 65 or over on 8 April 2013.

DLA is divided into two parts:
- a mobility component – for help with walking difficulties, paid at two rates, higher and lower
- a care component – for disabled children needing extra personal care or supervision because of a disability or long-term health condition, paid at three rates, higher, middle and lower.

You can claim by calling:
Ⓣ 0845 712 3456;
textphone 0845 722 4433

PERSONAL INDEPENDENCE PAYMENT

Personal Independence Payment (PIP) is a benefit for people who have a physical or mental disability and need help participating in everyday life or find it difficult to get around.

It replaces Disability Living Allowance (DLA) for people aged 16 or over. People under 65 who already get DLA will be asked to claim PIP instead. If you had reached the age of 65 by 8 April 2013, you can keep and renew your DLA award and won't be asked to claim PIP instead.

PIP is tax free, is not means tested and you do not need to have paid National Insurance contributions to be entitled to it. It is not affected by earnings or other income. It is almost always paid in full on top of other social security benefits or tax credits.

PIP has two components:
- a daily living component – for help participating in everyday life
- a mobility component – for help with getting around.

You can be paid either the daily living component or the mobility component on its own, or both components at the same time.

Each component is paid at two different levels: a 'standard rate' and an 'enhanced rate'.

PIP is for you, not for a carer. You can qualify for PIP whether or not you have someone helping you; what matters are the effects of your disability or health condition and the help you need, not whether you already get that help. You can spend your PIP on anything you like. PIP also acts as a 'passport' for other types of help.

You can claim by calling:
- ☎ 0800 917 2222
  textphone 0800 917 7777

For further information about DLA and PIP, including eligibility and current rates, refer to other Disability Rights UK guides, such as: *Claiming PIP* and the *Disability Rights Handbook*.
- Ⓦ www.disabilityrightsuk.org

Technology and equipment

Our quality of life and our choices often rely on finding smart solutions to meet our needs. Innovations in technology, equipment and design have developed at a rapid pace in the last decade, helping people with the spectrum of challenges that health conditions and disabilities may raise.

Innovation

Technology and equipment have been very liberating for many people with health conditions and disabilities.

Mobile phone use is only 25 years old and there have been other incredible developments in a relatively short time. For example, in the last 10 years, many people have moved away from desktop computers to mobile devices. Today's smartphones are mini-computers with an increasing range of features for people with a range of conditions, such as hearing or sight impairments, learning disabilities or memory or organisation challenges.

Devices can talk (including to each other), hook up to hearing aids, remind you of things, order your food and close your curtains. There is an incredible array of ingenious accessibility functions – and with help, almost anyone, of any age, can learn to use them.

We have recently seen the beginnings of 'smart' glasses. Google Glasses, which are hands-free, perched at ear, eye and mouth level, have the power of a mobile phone.

These technolgies hold real promise for helping people with particular disabilities.

Facial recognition software could identify how the person in front of you is feeling and flash up captions which say "happy", "sad" or "upset". This could be helpful for someone who finds it difficult to read emotions in others, such as people on the autism spectrum.

Deaf people could enjoy real-time subtitles so they can see what people are saying to them, as they can with television subtitles.

Increasingly, paralysed people can control computers and prostheses with their minds.

The most successful interface at the moment is an invasive one, where you undergo surgery and have things implanted in your brain. This is a very accurate technique. You can see videos (on the internet) of people who have had this procedure, with a robotic arm, drinking their cup of coffee.

Robin Christopherson, AbilityNet

Cathy Hutchinson using her thoughts to control a robotic arm and bring a flask of coffee to her mouth said:

"I couldn't believe my eyes when I was able to drink coffee without help. I was ecstatic. I had feelings of hope and a great sense of independence."

It was the first time in nearly 15 years that she had taken a drink unaided. She communicates by picking out letters on a board using eye movement.

There are apps available to tell us when the next bus is coming – very useful for people with visual impairments, for example.

GPS (satellite navigation) can be helpful if you experience anxiety when you are going somewhere new for the first time.

There are many organising facilities on smart phones that can help people with dyspraxia and dementia to remember things and run their lives.

Driverless cars are also on the horizon and are likely to cost about £5,000-£10,000 more than a regular family car.

Google Ventures – venture capitalists – have put in $258 million to purchase 25,000 autonomous taxis.

Robin Christopherson, AbilityNet.

Mobile phones and glasses are everyday mass-produced technologies and are more likely to be adopted than experimental, expensive devices made especially for the 'disabled market'.

Try searching the app store on your device for useful apps, many of them are free.

A techie tale
"On my phone I've got an app called 'talking goggles', which performs real-time object recognition."

Robin Christopherson of AbilityNet is blind and a disability tech enthusiast. He is looking forward to a time when this functionality could be constantly working for him in the form of smart glasses.

With greater choice and an ever-widening range of solutions to improve your standard of living, you need to be able to select the equipment that is most suited to your needs, then pinpoint and secure funding to pay for it.

Learning from people like us

There are lots of sources of advice on technology and equipment. Contact your local disabled people's organisation or centre for independent living to learn from people with similar experiences.

Independent living centres offer impartial advice on equipment for disabled people and display a range of products and information. Many also run training days, produce leaflets and provide other services. Some centres operate as retail outlets, so following an independent assessment you can buy the right equipment at the same place.

State provision

Local authorities or the NHS can provide much of the daily living or health-related equipment you will need.

To find out about local authority provision, contact a social worker or occupational therapist. Social care departments can provide advice as part of their assessment of your needs and through community occupational therapy services.

Daily living equipment includes:
- products for personal care and hygiene
- those that assist in using the bath or toilet, for example grab rails, bath boards and raised toilet seats
- products for food preparation, for example lever taps, adapted kitchen utensils
- products to help with the use of beds and chairs, for example bed raisers and rising/reclining chairs.

For NHS items, including wheelchairs, walking aids or communication aids, contact your GP.

Community Equipment Services bring together provision of social care and health equipment in England.

A kid's tale

Thomas was recently provided with some specialised crockery and cutlery to help him eat independently. However, he didn't want to use it because he wanted the same knives, forks and plates as his brothers.

Thomas's parents bought a 'plateguard' to try instead of his specialised plate. The plateguard clips onto standard crockery and provides a wall that food can be pushed up against. This also stops food from spilling off of the plate and onto the table.

The cutlery that Thomas had been provided with has built-up handles and no other special features. So, Thomas' parents bought foam tubing to build up the handles of their standard cutlery. This means that Thomas can use the same cutlery as his brothers.

Although his crockery and cutlery are adapted to his needs, Thomas is much happier. He can eat independently using the same stuff as the rest of the family and this has brought relative peace back to mealtimes!

Equipment may also be supplied for use in education and employment. Your GP or local authority should be able to provide you with more information.

This NHS website will help you find out about what's available in your local area to help you live independently:

Ⓦ www.nhs.uk/Service-Search/
Support-for-independent-living/
LocationSearch/386

Things to buy

Many high street shops and websites sell easy to use equipment – and you can see how other people have rated them. Some of them give you more choice about the style and look of the products.

You may decide to buy a product yourself or you may prefer to have a professional assessment if you are not quite sure what will work best. You may be able to use a personal health or social care budget to pay for this.

If you feel you need specialist equipment to help you manage more safely and easily around your home, you can contact the social care department of your local council and ask for a needs assessment.

They will usually arrange for you to have an assessment in your home by a social worker or an occupational therapist (OT). You do not have to have a letter from your doctor supporting your needs but this can sometimes speed up the process. Certain types of equipment may also be provided via health professionals such as physiotherapists and nurses.

Social care departments have a legal duty to make arrangements for the provision of services to support disabled people. If you are disabled or appear to have disability related needs, the social care department should not refuse to assess your need for possible service provision.

If your assessed needs meet local eligibility criteria, you will have a right to services that help to meet those needs, which may include disability equipment, which should be free of charge.

EQUIPMENT TO MEET HEALTH-RELATED NEEDS

Some items of equipment, such as a commode or a walking aid, will meet both health and domestic daily living needs. Your GP or a district nurse may arrange for you to receive these items or they may suggest you approach your social care department for a broader assessment of your needs.

Walking equipment can be provided following an assessment by a physiotherapist, who will be able to recommend the most appropriate aid and will make sure you know how to use it safely.

The Disabled Living Foundation produces a factsheet called *Choosing walking equipment*. This and other advice about things to consider when choosing daily living equipment can be downloaded from:
Ⓦ www.dlf.org.uk

If you have hearing problems and might benefit from a hearing aid, contact your GP who may refer you to your local hospital for a hearing test. You have a right to have your hearing assessed, particularly if you think your hearing loss is becoming a problem. The NHS issues hearing aids on loan free of charge.

If you have sight problems, low vision aids may help. Low vision services are usually located in hospital eye departments. They can make magnifiers and other low vision aids available on loan.

Your local social care department may provide a range of support services or employ specialist social workers to help people with sight or hearing loss.

Some items (including wigs and spinal supports) could be issued on an NHS prescription, for which there may be a charge (depending on where in the UK you live). If you are on a low income, you may qualify for help with these charges under the NHS Low Income scheme. See the chapter on money for details.

Technology in delivering services

The NHS is increasingly embracing technology to deliver services, from booking appointments and ordering repeat prescriptions online, to email contact with GP and skype consultations. In the future we will be able to access our own health records online.

The Choose and Book service enables you to book initial hospital appointments online in consultation with your GP.
Ⓦ www.chooseandbook.nhs.uk

"The Choose and Book system is a radical improvement on the old paper system. As a busy professional, I need to manage my time carefully. Choose and Book made it so much easier to book an appointment and made sure that I got one that fitted in well with my busy schedule."

It felt like a service that can accommodate my needs as an individual and not something I have to fall in line with.

Thinking about your needs

When you are beginning to consider the things you might need help with, AskSARA, an interactive resource from the Disabled Living Foundation, is a very useful place to start.

You can explore some of the challenges you are facing by filling in an online questionnaire and there is a telephone helpline. The resource will help you find out about the types of equipment that are available or changes you might need to make to your home.

📞 0300 999 0004 (helpline)
   Monday to Friday 10am-4pm
🌐 http://asksara.dlf.org.uk

There are lots of equipment providers in the market and getting independent, impartial advice is really important. The Disabled Living Foundation offers advice on where to find suitable providers.
🌐 www.dlf.org.uk

Another useful website with information about equipment is Really Useful Stuff.
🌐 www.reallyusefulstuff.co

You can also get help via a social care assessment and from an occupational therapist. See the chapter on health and social care for further details.

Using a computer at home

Before you consider investing in new technology, there are many things you can do to adapt your home computer and enable accessibility features already built in.

My Computer My Way shows you how you can select features to help with sight, sound, keyboard, mouse or understanding.
🌐 www.abilitynet.org.uk/advice-info/
   my-computer-my-way

If you decide you need more specialised assistance, AbilityNet has a library of factsheets which cover technologies and solutions available for a wide range of learning and physical disabilities. They provide detailed information on a wide range of assistive technology and include step-by-step guides to help you set up your computer and software to meet your individual requirements.
🌐 www.abilitynet.org.uk/factsheets

The BBC has produced an accessibility guide on using computers and the internet, including details of how to set up voice-recognition software.
🌐 www.bbc.co.uk/accessibility

Further information
Organisations that can help with hardware, software, training and consultancy solutions at home and at work:
🌐 www.abilitynet.org.uk
🌐 www.adapt-it.co.uk
🌐 www.livingmadeeasy.org.uk
🌐 www.assist-it.org.uk
🌐 www.lcdisability.org

Adapting your home

Depending on your needs you may want to make some changes at home to ensure you are able to continue living there independently.

This could mean widening doorways, adding a stair-lift or a downstairs bathroom, adapting heating and lighting controls to make them accessible, or changing your kitchen appliances, cupboards or work surface heights.

Most areas have a home improvement service to help with quick repairs or small adaptations like grab rails. They can also help get grants for bigger adaptations.

Many also offer 'handy person services' to put in safety features and help make sure homes are suitable to return to after a spell in hospital.

To find your local service visit the national body for Home Improvement Agency and Handypersons Services:
Ⓦ www.foundations.uk.com

You can apply for a government grant to help you pay for these changes:
Ⓦ www.gov.uk/disabled-facilities-grants

Smarter living by design

There is an ever-increasing array of products available to make your life easier and safer at home.

Telecare personal alarms let you alert someone if there's something wrong, by pressing a button on a wristband or pendant.

Tehream is a single mum who cares for her sons (aged seven and 12) who are severely autistic and profoundly deaf. Her younger child is currently in foster care with regular home visits. Tehream had not had a full night's sleep for 10 years and was finding it increasingly difficult to manage as her sons grew bigger and stronger. Her eldest son left the sink running and flooded the kitchen and both sons are prone to leaving the house by the windows and doors, causing danger to themselves.

A telecare solution that lets Tehream know as soon as an incident occurs, via a pager during the day and an under-pillow vibrator at night has helped enormously. The solution includes:
- A bed occupancy sensor for each of the boys' beds. If they get out of bed in the night and don't return within a preset period of time, Tehream is woken.
- Flood detectors in the kitchen and bathroom.
- Exit sensors on the door to the property and the windows.

With these in place, if the boys leave the house, Tehream's is alerted via the pager or under pillow vibrator. She says: "I have been able to get a good night's sleep for the first time in many years, as I no longer have to stay awake at night worrying about my sons' activities. I also know I'm not completely alone in caring for my children. They would both be in foster care if it wasn't for telecare".

Jacob is six years old and loves sport and computer games. He has epilepsy and can experience a seizure at any time day or night. He lives with his parents.

Jacob has always slept in his parents' bedroom so that they can attend to him if he has a seizure during the night. His mum frequently sleeps in Jacob's bed as she is anxious that he may have a seizure without her hearing. Both Jacob and his parents are keen that he should now have his own bedroom. However, his parents need to know if Jacob experiences a seizure during the night.

A telecare solution was installed including a telecare control box and personal alarm button so Jacob's mum can call for help and support at any time. An epilepsy sensor has been placed on Jacob's bed. This will detect if he experiences a seizure whilst in his bed. A vibrating pager and a vibrating disc are kept by Jacob's parents' bed. His mum keeps the vibrating disc under her pillow; if their son has a seizure she is woken immediately via the pager and disc.

Jacob's mum says: "This has given us peace of mind and reduced the anxiety and sleepless nights. We are now able to sleep in our own bed again, knowing we will be alerted when our son has an epileptic seizure during the night. It has also given me more time to spend with my other child during the day."

Motion sensors can be used to raise an alarm or make falls less likely by automatically switching on lights.

To help in the kitchen, there are clamps to open jars or bottles, one-handed salt and pepper mills, easy-grip handles for utensils, rotating mug handles and talking gadgets to help you weigh ingredients or time your cooking.

Audio or smart labelling systems can help you store and find things – not just in the kitchen but all around your home.

You can buy trolleys, trays and carrying devices of all sizes to enable you to take your belongings with you as you need them.

Smart storage is available, including pull-down wardrobe rails, which will fit into your existing furniture.

If you have difficulty opening doors, turning keys or hearing the doorbell, you can choose from a range of security, intercoms and assistive equipment to improve access to your own home.

The Disabled Living Foundation Supplier Directory provides an extensive list of providers to cater to your needs at home.
Ⓦ www.dlfdirectory.org.uk

There is more information on using technology and equipment at home in the at home chapter.

Communicating with others

Being able to get in touch with friends, organise appointments, manage your working life or call for help in emergency is essential to maintaining your independence.

BT has a number of services and products to assist people who have problems with communications. Large button landlines and mobile handsets are now widely available.
ⓦ www.btplc.com/inclusion

Action on Hearing Loss provides advice on amplified telephone equipment, minicoms or textphones.
ⓦ www.actiononhearingloss.org.uk

The RNIB has useful information on using phones, computers and mobile devices if you have a visual impairment.
ⓦ www.rnib.org.uk

Eileen is 87 and has early onset dementia. She uses technology to remind her to take the tablets she needs that delay the development of her dementia and for her heart condition.

She is used to being independent and is still physically mobile. Her daughter provides support such as shopping and lives nearby.

Eileen likes to walk to her local shops every day to get some fresh air, talk to the shopkeepers and buy her own milk. A device fixed to her coat helps her daughter find her if she gets lost, giving them both peace of mind.

Netbuddy provides tips and peer expertise for people with a learning disability, autism or special needs. It includes links to blogs, apps and equipment that can enhance communication using symbols and visual-supports, as well as apps to help with social networking.
ⓦ www.netbuddy.org.uk

Communication aids help people to communicate more effectively with those around them. Aids range from simple letter boards to sophisticated computer equipment. They are of particular use for people who are non-speakers. For more information, visit the ACE Centre website.
ⓦ http://acecentre.org.uk

Paying for equipment

You may be able to get state assistance to pay for some of the equipment you need. For information on assessments and government funding visit:
ⓦ www.gov.uk/browse/disabilities/ equipment

VAT relief on equipment

If you're disabled or have a long-term illness, you won't be charged VAT on products designed or adapted for your own personal or domestic use. This includes installation, repairs or maintenance, spare parts or accessories.

You qualify if:
- you have a physical or mental impairment that affects your ability to carry out everyday activities
- you have a condition that's treated as chronic sickness
- you're terminally ill.

You'll need to confirm in writing that you meet these conditions. You don't qualify if you're temporarily disabled or elderly but non-disabled.

Qualifying products or services

Products designed or adapted for a disability usually qualify, for example, certain types of:
- adjustable beds
- stair lifts
- wheelchairs
- medical appliances to help with severe injuries
- alarms
- braille paper or low vision aids – (not spectacles or contact lenses)
- motor vehicles – or the leasing of a motability vehicle.

For more information contact HMRC:
- ☎ 0300 123 1073 (choose option 1)
- Ⓦ www.hmrc.gov.uk/charities/vat-relief-disabled.htm

You may be able to use your personal health budget to buy equipment that promotes your health and wellbeing.

> Personal health budgets in England are for people who are eligible for NHS Continuing Healthcare. Clinicians can also offer them to other people that they feel may benefit from the additional flexibility and control.
>
> A personal health budget is an amount of money to support the identified healthcare and wellbeing needs of an individual, which is planned and agreed between the individual, or their representative, and the local clinical commissioning group (CCG).

Some types of equipment are available on loan so you can try before you make a purchase. For information visit:
- Ⓦ www.dlf.org.uk/library

Local Red Cross branches run a short-term medical equipment loan service for wheelchairs, mobility aids and other equipment.
- Ⓦ www.redcross.org.uk

Second-hand equipment

Organisations that can help you access good quality second-hand equipment:
- Ⓦ www.otstores.co.uk
- Ⓦ www.scope.org.uk/support/disabled-people/independent-living/used-equipment
- Ⓦ www.disabledgear.com
- Ⓦ www.askdes.org.uk
- Ⓦ www.disabledliving.co.uk/Home

Equipped for life

Technology and universal design are improving every area of our lives, making the world more accessible to people with a wide range of different abilities and circumstances.

Paying for services and goods on a daily basis is becoming easier for us all with cashless and mobile systems being introduced on buses and trains, parking and for small purchases in shops.

Technology and design have significantly enhanced public transport services, from step-free access, audio and visual information and announcements, hearing loops at stations, tactile surfaces and colour coding.

This online guide by Transport for London helps to explain how technology is making the London Underground more accessible.
ⓦ www.tfl.gov.uk/transport-accessibility

Enabled by Design is an online community critiquing the best and worst of assistive design and technology.
ⓦ www.enabledbydesign.org

The National Autistic Society produces a useful guide for people living with autism. It provides helpful tips to deal with day-to-day tasks including shopping, appointments, local journeys, holidays and becoming a driver. There is also information about using technology for leisure, communication and social activities in the *Living with autism* section of their website.
ⓦ www.autism.org.uk

Technology training

There are lots of ways in which you might improve your skills as a user of technology. Some of this may relate to acquiring a disability or health condition.

Some local authorities offer specialist rehabilitation services such as Rehabilitation Officers for Visual Impairment to support blind people.

There is a training element to the Access to Work scheme (see the chapter on learning and working).

Many adult education courses focus on improving internet and other technical skills. There is voluntary sector support as well.

The Tinder Foundation supports people to use digital technology. It has a network of 5,000 local community partners and a Community *How To* website. It manages the UK online centres network and the Learn My Way online learning platform. So far, the Foundation has helped more than 1 million people gain the skills they need to use computers and the internet confidently.
ⓦ www.tinderfoundation.org

Learning online

An online learning community is a public or private place on the internet that addresses the learning needs of its members by facilitating peer-to-peer learning.

Through social networking and computer-mediated communication, people can work together to achieve a shared learning objective. This offers huge potential to people with health conditions or disabilities who find travelling to study too tiring, painful or expensive.

Learning objectives may be proposed by the community owner or may arise out of discussions between participants that reflect personal interests. In an online learning community, people share knowledge via text discussion (either in 'real time' or when it's convenient to reply), audio, video, or other internet-supported media.

Blogs where people share their ideas and information, often on sites with others, blend personal reflection with social networking.

eTwinning, for example, is a European online community operated by European schoolnet comprising more than 50,000 registered teachers.

Types of online learning communities include e-learning communities (groups interact and connect solely via technology) and blended learning communities (groups use face-to-face meetings as well as online meetings). Online learning communities can be knowledge-based, practice-based or task-based.

Some communities use course management tools (such as Dokeos, eFront, Claroline, Moodle, Chamilo, Lectureshare or OpenLearning).

Massive open online course (MOOC) is an online learning model designed to offer unlimited participation and open access via the internet. In addition to traditional course materials such as videos, readings, and problem sets, MOOCs provide interactive user forums that help build a community for students, professors, and teaching assistants. MOOCs are a recent development in distance education which began to emerge in 2012.
ⓦ www.massiveopenonlinecourses.com

ShowMe is an open online learning community where anyone can learn and teach any topic. Its iPad app lets you easily create and share video lessons:
ⓦ www.showme.com

YouTube also includes a wide range of online learning resources:
ⓦ www.youtube.com

Designing, commissioning and making technology

What about creating a custom-made prosthetic limb or a chair that is comfortable because it is made precisely to your measurements? At some point in the future we may be able to go online and commission bespoke technology in a global market for innovation and design.

Dad Richard Pollins, who was born without legs, told the Guardian newspaper about his use of equipment to help with parenting; some of it cobbled together, some of it high-tech and some of it using something that's out there already for all parents.

"Anyone who has had a baby will know how much kit they come with. It turns out that being a parent with no legs just means having more kit. At the low end of the scale, I initially used a bucket tray on wheels, stuffed with a changing mat for comfort. If I put the baby in the bucket tray, I could push him from room to room. It was a highly effective and cheap solution and Joseph found it fun.

As for the high end, I was very grateful for the effort, thought and funding that went into producing a special chair that I keep by Joseph's cot. The chair, which is moulded to fit my torso, is powered to lift me from floor level to above the cot and, strapped in with Velcro, I can tilt myself almost 30 degrees, so that I can safely pick up the baby with both hands.

We will be able to share our designs via open source software and make new designs and prototypes using digital fabrication. An example of developments in this area is the 'Machines Room', a new community 'fab lab', where you can hire equipment by the hour or pay staff to print prototypes for designs of your own, including 3-D printing.

Ⓦ http://machinesroom.org/about

It is very clever and a real game-changer, allowing me to care for my child in our home alone. At first, Joseph was less grateful – regularly bursting into tears at the sound of the Velcro strapping being ripped apart. I tried ripping it slowly and softly, getting it over with as quickly as possible, even singing over the noise. Eventually, he got used to it.

Occasionally, I have managed to carry Joseph outside. I have tried using a baby carrier a few times; I strapped him on me while we were on the floor and then tried to get myself into my legs, but Joseph was blocking my view, which made it very tricky. I managed, but it was more luck than judgment.

I also have a special jogger contraption – designed for keen keep-fit parents – that attaches to the buggy, so I can push it using my stomach. We also road-tested a baby carrier that goes on your back, and Joseph loved being able to hit me over the head while I stomped around. Unfortunately, I couldn't put the carrier on or take it off without help so it has limited use."

Technology to help you get and keep a job

When a disability or health condition starts or worsens, there can be an impact on whether you can still do the same job or how you do it. Technology can make a huge difference. For example, voice-activated software for people who use computers in their work can mean you can continue using them if you lose your sight or dexterity. The Access to Work scheme is designed to help people with disabilities and health conditions stay in work or move into work. It can pay for the cost of work-related technology and training. There are further details in the chapter on learning and working.

Your rights

The Equality Act 2010 gives you rights in the way you use services or receive goods. Anyone who provides a service to the public, or a section of the public, is a service provider – and this includes private landlords, housing associations, local authorities, restaurants, cinemas and shops. Providers need to make reasonable adjustments so you can use their services – if they don't they may be in breach of the law.

If you think you may have been discriminated against and would like to make a complaint you have a number of options.

If you have a complaint about a local authority, you should make your complaint directly to them. If you do not get a satisfactory resolution, you can take your complaint to the Local Government Ombudsman.
Ⓦ www.lgo.org.uk

If you have a complaint about a housing association or a local authority housing provider, you should lodge a complaint with them directly. If your complaint is not dealt with to your satisfaction you can go to the Housing Ombudsman. Some private landlords are also registered with this body.
Ⓦ www.housing-ombudsman.org.uk

The Equality and Human Rights Commission has advice on considering which process to follow depending on the nature of your complaint, including a helpline.
Ⓦ www.equalityhumanrights.com

The Equality Advisory Support Service and the Citizens Advice Bureau can advise you on how to pursue a complaint about discrimination.
Ⓦ www.equalityadvisoryservice.com
Ⓦ www.adviceguide.org.uk

The Law Centres Network set up across parts of the UK can provide you with impartial legal advice.
Ⓦ www.lawcentres.org.uk

The arbitration service ACAS can help with complaints relating to work or employment.
Ⓦ www.acas.org.uk

Disability Rights UK provides advice on your rights and how to make a complaint in this useful factsheet:
Ⓦ www.disabilityrightsuk.org/making-complaint

Health and social care services

Health and social care services are crucial but they are the means to an end – the chance to lead the life you want. These services should enable people with long-term conditions and disabilities to take part in family and community life, to work if feasible and to enjoy other activities.

For many of us, it is only by taking charge of health and social care services that we can have the life we want.

Independent living

Most of us need to visit a doctor or dentist from time to time and we may need hospital treatment too. Some of us rely on both health and social care services for help with long-term health conditions or impairments.

CHOOSING YOUR SUPPORT

The idea of independent living emphasises choice and control; that people with health conditions and disabilities are the experts on our own needs and have valuable perspectives to contribute to society.

We should be able to decide how to live, work, and take part in our communities and have the choice of services that affect our day-to-day lives.

The essence of independent living is the freedom to make decisions about your own life and to participate fully in your community. John Evans, one of the founders of the independent living movement.

Disability Rights UK defines independent living as follows: "Independent living means being able to live in the way you choose, with people you choose. It means having choices about who helps you and the ways they help. It is not necessarily about doing things for yourself. It is about having control over your day-to-day life."

Taking charge

Health and social care services
Ask yourself the following questions:
- How can services help me lead the life I want?
- What are all the options available?
- What am I entitled to?
- What would suit me best?
- Who can help me decide?
- What's worked well for other people? Not just people I know but other people in similar circumstances?

Social care services are arranged by local authorities in England, Scotland and Wales and health and social care boards in Northern Ireland. They come in many forms and are provided by public, private and voluntary organisations. Services include support for people with mental health conditions, older and disabled people, mostly in our own homes but sometimes in residential and nursing homes.

PERSONALISATION

One of the big recent changes in both health and social care has been a focus on 'personalisation' which puts you at the centre of the process of identifying your needs and making choices about how you are supported.

Self-directed support is a key part of personalisation. It increases your opportunity to choose the social and health support that works best for you. Often this happens through a personal budget and direct payments – so you can decide on and buy the most appropriate personal support and longer term health support for you.

The National Health Service (NHS) is the four publicly funded healthcare systems in England, Northern Ireland, Scotland and Wales. They provide a comprehensive range of health services, the vast majority of which are free at the point of use for people legally resident in the United Kingdom.

The NHS exists to promote health and wellbeing for everyone. People with health conditions and disabilities are often frequent users of NHS services. It helps to have the information and the confidence to negotiate for high-quality and timely care.

Personalisation
The process by which health and social care services can be adapted to suit you

Self-directed support
Your active involvement in decisions about the support you get and how the budget is spent

Personal health budget
The amount of money your local NHS team allocates to meet your health and wellbeing needs

Personal budget
The amount of money your local authority allocates to meet your social care and support needs

---

GETTING THE SUPPORT YOU NEED

In recent years there have been a number of changes to the way social care needs are assessed, who is eligible and how services are paid for.

There are differences across England, Northern Ireland, Scotland and Wales in who is eligible and how social care is funded and provided. Local or national disability organisations within the four UK countries and your local authority/ health and social care board can provide more information.

Personal budgets for social care

A personal budget for social care (an individual budget in Scotland) sets out the amount of money allocated to cover the costs of your social care and support needs.

The amount is based on a support plan agreed between you and your local authority.

You can receive the money as a direct payment, ask your local authority to organise the services for you, arrange for a third party to manage the budget on your behalf or use a combination.

To find out more:
ⓦ www.disabilityrightsuk.org/
 personal-budgets

Personal health budgets

Personal health budgets work in a similar way to the personal budgets that many people are already using to manage their social care and support needs.

While services may come from a variety of organisations, different services are beginning to work more effectively together, to consider people 'in the round' and to take account of what people want from life, not just what their medical needs are.

Independent living enables us as disabled people to achieve our own goals and live our own lives in the way that we choose for ourselves.

A personal health budget sets out the amount of money allocated to cover your NHS health and wellbeing needs. It is planned and agreed between you and your local NHS team.

They were introduced in 2014 for people eligible for NHS Continuing Healthcare (NHS-funded long-term health and personal care provided outside hospital). They are now being extended to give more people with long-term conditions and disabilities greater choice and control over the healthcare they receive.

If you choose to receive a personal health budget and a personal budget for social care, it may be possible to combine the two budgets. In some areas, the assessment, planning and review processes may also be dealt with jointly.

To find out more:
ⓦ www.nhs.uk/
 personalhealthbudgets

What is a direct payment?

Once your local authority agrees that you are eligible for care and support and has set a personal budget, you will be asked whether you want the services to be arranged by the local authority on your behalf or would prefer to buy them yourself. You can choose to have some services provided directly by social care and others arranged by yourself using a direct payment.

A direct payment is money paid directly to you by the local authority, according to your personal budget, and can be used by you to purchase any services which meet your assessed care needs.

People receiving social care services are automatically entitled to direct payments but you cannot be forced to have them. They may give you more control over the way your care needs are met. You can buy services (eg employing your own personal assistants), equipment or respite care that you have been assessed as needing.

Direct payments cannot be used to purchase care in a care home, apart from periods of up to four weeks respite care (120 days for children) in any one year.

In England and Wales: To get a direct payment you must be one of the following:
- a disabled person
- a carer

- a person with parental responsibility for a child with a disability.

You must also be aged 16 or over and assessed as needing community care services or services as a carer. You must be willing to have direct payments and be able to manage them (alone or with assistance).

In England and Wales, direct payments have been extended to people who lack the mental capacity to agree to and manage direct payments themselves: payments can now be made to a willing and appropriate person on the disabled person's behalf. See Mental Capacity Act in Your rights at the end of this chapter if your capacity is questioned.

You cannot have direct payments if you are subject to criminal justice legislation.

In Northern Ireland: You are eligible to receive direct payments if you are over 16 and have been assessed as needing personal social services. This includes carers.

In Scotland: You can get direct payments if you are assessed as needing an eligible care service. There are some exceptions to this. Carers do not receive services in their own right so cannot get direct payments for caring. If you cannot give consent or manage your affairs, a representative can receive and manage direct payments on your behalf.

Policy-makers increasingly talk about 'integration', which means health and social care working together to meet people's needs.

We are going to set out the biggest offer to bring health and social care together that there's been since 1948 – a new option for combining them at the level of the individual.

Simon Stevens, CEO, NHS England.

Taking charge

With personal budgets

Here are some examples of the ways people have spent their health or social care personal budgets:

- employing a personal assistant (someone who will work with you to help you live independently and do the things you want)
- buying medical equipment to use at home
- using alternative therapies
- learning to play a musical instrument
- paying for counselling
- going to the theatre, cinema or a museum
- joining a gym
- getting a computer and using the internet
- going on a short break or holiday
- paying for your train, tram and bus fares
- getting a job
- seeing friends or meeting new people
- going to a place of worship
- buying a bike to get healthy and go to college or work.

One of the best ways to learn how to navigate the system is to learn from others who have done so before you. You can search for the contact details of your local disabled people's organisation that provides support services on the NHS Choices website:

- Ⓦ www.nhs.uk/Service-Search/ Support-for-independent-living/ LocationSearch/386

Self-directed support

For more information visit:

- Ⓦ www.disabilityrightsuk.org/ community-care-direct-payments
- Ⓦ www.selfdirectedsupportscotland. org.uk

I like the flexibility that self-directed support gives you, as I feel it is important to be able to use different approaches and ideas with different people, unlike traditional services. I think you need to get the holistic picture of a person and think outside the box to find out what people would like and what would be best to suit their needs.

Your rights

Social care

In England: The Care Act 2014 provides for anyone to have an assessment, even if you think you may have too much money to receive support from your local authority. The Care Act says that you should receive advice and information from the local authority and that you have to have 'substantial' needs to access support from the local authority.

In Northern Ireland: If you have been assessed as needing social care services, these are free at the point of need. You can receive these directly from the health and social care board or in the form of a direct payment to choose and buy the services yourself.

In Scotland: Self-directed support is the policy in Scotland. Older people don't pay for personal care but, in common with others who need social care support, do have to pay for help at home or to do things outside the home.
- Ⓦ www.selfdirectedsupportscotland.org.uk

In Wales: The Welsh Government has recently launched a new independent living strategy. In Wales, the maximum anyone has to pay for social care support at home is £55 a week, whatever their level of need.
- Ⓦ www.disabilitywales.org/social-model/independent-living

Support at home and with activities

Social care services may include:
- personal care at home
- support to get out and about
- care in residential or nursing homes
- domestic help
- help with meals
- provision of equipment.

In 2013-14, 1,267,000 people in England were receiving social care support. Resources are limited and cuts to social care budgets mean there is increasing pressure on public bodies' ability to meet costs.

Local authorities (in England, Scotland and Wales) and health and social care boards (in Northern Ireland) are responsible for assessing for and arranging social care. They can charge for services or they can give a direct payment (although you may still have to cover some of the cost) so you can buy the care you need independently.

Disablity Rights UK and other organisations are campaigning to increase eligibility under the Care Act so that more people can benefit, at an earlier stage.

Portability
Portability of social care, the ability to transfer a package of services from one area to another, was recognised by the Care Act 2014. This is an important principle, helping people to move for a variety of reasons, including taking up a job or being closer to family.

GETTING AN ASSESSMENT

The first step is to ask your local authority social care department for an assessment of your needs.

The government's website will help you find contact details for your local authority so you can request a social care assessment.

Ⓦ www.gov.uk/apply-needs-assessment-social-services

Your local authority should:
- assess your needs and give you advice, whatever your financial circumstances
- tell you about local services and who to contact locally for advice
- be able to provide information about services and support options available to you in your area
- give you relevant information if you are an unpaid/family carer.

Your rights

Local authorities have a duty to assess anyone who appears to need the social care services they offer. This includes disabled adults and children and people who provide unpaid support (carers).

The assessment helps work out what your difficulties are and what services will help you most. Each local authority has its own way of working out who is eligible for social care support and what services it can offer. You will be asked to provide financial information as well.

Ⓦ www.nhs.uk/CarersDirect/social-care/Pages/what-social-care-support-can-get.aspx

You have the right to be assessed for local authority care services. Whether or not you get any of these services depends on the outcome of a 'social care assessment' and your financial situation.

Personal support for children
Each local authority has staff dealing specifically with social care for children.

If you think your child would benefit from additional support, you might want to speak to your child's GP or teacher first. If you or your child needs more significant support, contact the children's services team in your local authority for a needs assessment.

This assessment of your child's needs will be used to determine if they need more specialised support. You should be involved in any decisions about your child, including what help will be provided to meet their needs.

After an assessment

If your local authority thinks you are eligible for social care support, you have a specific level of need and meet financial rules, you should then be involved in the decision-making process that follows.

The next step would be for social care or an independent adviser to work with you to create a care and support plan, which covers the full range of support or care you are eligible for.

 www.nhs.uk/CarersDirect/guide/assessments/Pages/Thecareplan.aspx

For many of us, just a bit of help is needed – such as meals on wheels or help with washing or dressing. Yet these services could make a big difference to your life.

If you feel that your needs have changed over time, you can be re-assessed. Contact the social care team at your local authority to discuss it with them.

Taking charge

Not just alive but a life
Make sure when you are having an assessment and in planning your care, that you emphasise the things you enjoy – the life you want to lead.

For example, you may have recently been diagnosed with dementia – you can still go fishing or meet friends, perhaps using a personal budget to pay for any extra support you need. You may have a learning disability and need support to go to work.

SOCIAL CARE PLANNING

A person-centred plan should take into account not only your health but also your personal, family, social, economic, educational, mental health, ethnic and cultural background and circumstances.

It should also focus on what you want your care to achieve, for example to help you live independently, achieve at school or return to work.

"I'm 84 and I've always loved the outdoors. When I was younger I was in the Ramblers Association. Now I've got dementia. At first, I was isolated and housebound. I was referred to a specialist dementia home care service by my local community psychiatric nurse.

The person who saw me actually asked about me, my life, what's important to me, what sort of support I want.

Now I go out twice a week to the park. This is the highlight of my week. I feel so much better in myself. I look forward to my walks so much. It's independence, isn't it? And I'm used to that!"

Your plan is then paid for – either by you, using money (your direct payment) from social care services – or by the local authority.

In person-centered planning, the focus is on an individual and that person's vision of what they would like to do in the future rather than on what services are available.

Various services and staff plan and facilitate opportunities for someone to develop personal relationships, participate in their community and increase control over their own lives.

USING A DIRECT PAYMENT TO PAY FOR A PERSONAL ASSISTANT

Many people with health conditions and disabilities use personal assistants (PAs): people who help them with everyday tasks and support them to participate in all aspects of life.

The money for this can be used to employ a care agency, which means that the agency will have responsibility for all employment rules and procedures for the staff providing care.

However, if direct payment users employ staff directly, then they will be classed as an employer.

Employing a personal assistant

There are many benefits of employing a PA directly:

- they work for you
- you decide what you want them to do
- you decide when you want them to work.

If you or someone acting on your behalf employs staff directly, you are bound by all the laws that cover employment and are responsible for things like payroll, workplace insurance, health and safety and recruitment.

There should be some support available from local councils for general direct payment administration.

For employment administration, such as payroll and recruitment, you may be able to get help with this through local independent living projects.

The one thing that oppressed me for years was that other people thought they knew best about how I should live my life. Or not live it.

Baroness Campbell, disabled peer.

Recruiting a personal assistant

To employ a personal assistant, you will need to write a job description listing the tasks you would like them to do. You will need to include a person specification, describing the skills, qualities and experience you would like them to have.

You can advertise locally, shortlist candidates and carry out interviews. It is best to do this away from your own home and with a friend or adviser. Once you have offered the job to a successful candidate it is important that you check all references and keep a clear record of their recruitment and employment.

Skills for Care provides useful toolkit on creating a job description, how to recruit a PA, managing them once they are in post, training and qualifications, and resolving problems if they arise.

ⓦ www.skillsforcare.org.uk
ⓦ www.employingpersonalassistants.co.uk

Anne Pridmore lives in a small market town in the Midlands.

"I married in 1964, worked full-time and didn't recognise myself as a disabled person although I had never been able to walk. Twenty years later my partner left me, and I found myself at 44 years of age unable to do the most basic things for myself.

As I had three months' notice of his intention to leave, I contacted social services asking them for help. Three days before he was due to leave I found myself unable to go for a pee, get out of bed or into bed unaided. Social services visited me and told me that they didn't know what to do with me, and did I know of anyone who would 'look after me?'!

Between 1991 and 1993 I campaigned to persuade the local authority to allow me to swap services (home care, bath nurse, district nurses) for cash. This was my first step to liberation and the disabled people's movement. It was a long battle, but the end result meant that 35 disabled people in Leicestershire were able – for the first time – to have control over their lives through the use of third-party payments.

If your PA is an employee, you have more control as you decide the working hours, and are responsible for providing pay slips, paid holiday, a contract of employment, and sick pay. HM Revenue and Customs (HMRC) provides detailed advice on employment status.

ⓦ www.hmrc.gov.uk

With the introduction nationally of direct payments, the rest is history you might think. However, I have always felt that the most crucial criterion for a good personal assistant (PA) is the 'relationship' between you. It is easy to teach a person to cook your favourite meal, but getting the relationship right is more tricky. Understanding what makes a good PA and how to make the relationship work is often about having good ground rules. Even though I am an experienced PA user, I am still learning, and I certainly still continue to have problems recruiting and managing staff.

Whilst there is a lot of support available from service user-led organisations, peer support at a national level is very scarce. Even at a local level, many peer-support groups have now closed due to lack of funding.

I have therefore created the Being the Boss website to address the lack of peer support available to disabled people who employ our own Personal Assistants (PAs)."

To find out more:
ⓦ www.beingtheboss.co.uk

USEFUL CONTACTS

ACAS has helpful advice on resolving problems relating to employment
Ⓦ www.acas.org.uk

Being the Boss is a website that shares information based on the experiences of disabled people who employ PAs. They run a discussion and support forum and publish a handbook for disabled employers.
Ⓦ www.beingtheboss.co.uk

CHANGE is a leading national human rights organisation, working for the rights of all people with learning disabilities. They employ people with learning disabilities on an equal, living wage to produce accessible resources and deliver training.
Ⓦ www.changepeople.co.uk

Disability and Tax offers a series of helpful factsheets on: becoming an employer, tax, national insurance and keeping records.
Ⓦ www.disabilitytaxguide.org.uk/about/ resources

Find Me Good Care

The Social Care Institute for Excellence's Find Me Good Care website aims to help people make choices about care and support (in England). It includes advice and information about choosing care, a database of councils and a list of organisations providing advice and support services. There are links to specialist websites including independent financial advisors.
Ⓦ www.scie.org.uk/findmegoodcare

Independent Living Alternatives (ILA) is an organisation of disabled people providing a comprehensive range of personal assistance services. ILA aims to enable people who need personal assistance, to be able to live independently in the community and take full control of their lives and thereby have individuality and spontaneity. ILA either provides personal assistants or enables individuals to employ their own personal assistants.
Ⓦ www.ilanet.co.uk

PA Pool provides members with a browsable database of PAs and PA Users, including information about each person and who or what they are looking for.
Ⓦ www.papool.co.uk

PERS (Pay and Employment Rights Service) provides a range of free and affordable services on all aspects of employment law and good practice.
Ⓦ www.pers.org.uk

Some insurers offer insurance specifically for those using direct payments or a personal budget. It is worth checking carefully what is covered and comparing prices before taking out an insurance policy.

Roxburgh UK provides assistance, consultation and training to people who wish to live independently and to those working in the social care sector.
Ⓦ www.roxburghuk.com

Many local disabled people's organisations offer support to plan and manage your budget. For example:

Essex Coalition of Disabled People:
Ⓦ www.ecdp.org.uk
Spectrum in Southampton has a standalone website of support for managing direct payments:
Ⓦ http://directpaymentssouthampton. info

Check whether your local disabled people's organisation can provide support.

Help recruiting a personal assistant
Ⓦ www.carepair.co.uk
Ⓦ www.papool.co.uk
Ⓦ www.padatabase.org

The Disability Tax Guide, information for anyone taking on a personal assistant, is published by the Low Incomes Tax Reform Group:
Ⓦ www.disabilitytaxguide.org.uk

Independent living enables people such as me to learn, work, volunteer, play and live in a way that meets our needs and allows us to be full and active members of the society we live in.

Baroness Campbell, who has spinal muscular atrophy and uses full-time personal assistants.

MANAGING THE BUDGET

You can decide how to stay in control of your personal budget, and how to organise the support you need. You can do this through independent brokers, agents, trusts or through the local authority.

> Your support plan and personal budget will be reviewed regularly by social care to ensure it is working for you both now and in the future.

You can get your 'self-directed support' money as a direct payment if you want to manage (organise and pay for) your support yourself (though assistance in relation to recruitment and payroll can always be provided by a support agency).

> Susan Bick, from Scotland says: "I've got MS and I've had it for 33 years. Only in the last ten years has it really been a problem for me. My balance is the most badly affected thing. I don't go to work anymore and I don't drive. So direct payments are absolutely perfect for me because they get me out of the house. I receive direct payments from the social work department and they give me the ability to employ somebody myself. I've been getting direct payments for about two years now. Lizzie had been made redundant and it just worked out perfectly. I get Lizzie, my personal assistant, for nine hours a week. We go to college one day a week. We also go to yoga and Pilates a couple of other days. It relieves the pressure on my husband as well."

Or you can receive the funding as an indirect payment, ie another person or organisation manages the money on your behalf. You can also have a deputy or attorney to help you if you need it.

For more information
For information on managing your personal budget, read Disability Rights UK's factsheet:
- Ⓦ www.disabilityrightsuk.org/managing-your-personal-budget

For advice about personal budgets and personal health budgets contact our Self-Directed Support helpline:
- Ⓣ 0300 555 1525
- Ⓔ selfdirectedsupport@disabilityrightsuk.org

Social care 'brokers'

Lots of people use an insurance broker to help them get the best deal on car or household insurance – and to help them if things go wrong.

You can also get help with managing your personal budget and access relevant information through brokerage and advocacy services. Local support brokers can provide one-to-one support or additional continuous support for those who need it, or support by phone or online. Having a broker to help you manage your personal budget can help make the process a lot easier.

Good brokers are trained and are up-to-date with the social care and social security systems. They use their experience to help you source the best support solutions available to achieve maximum independence.

Your broker encourages you to take part in decision-making. You will be given time to think and express your opinion on decisions aimed at planning for the short and long term, as well as contingency plans.

Your broker acts as a neutral person avoiding giving a personal opinion and acts as a mediator to resolve any problems with other service providers.

As well as understanding your disability or health condition, needs and culture, brokers have the latest knowledge to make use of the best resources currently available to match your personal and financial circumstances.

A broker's duty is to make you feel valued and confident in decision-making. In addition, your broker can liaise with your personal support network (which could include family, friends, service providers and local funding agencies) to help you plan and manage your support solutions.

Those who access brokerage services are more likely to get good services. There is more chance for a support/action plan to be approved by social services if you get help from a broker who has specialist expertise in this field.

> Your broker can support you to write a self-directed action plan that suits your personal circumstances. A good broker considers your whole situation, including your cultural needs. They will work with you to plan how to achieve suitable support.

Brokers can be limited companies or operate as sole traders. They can work independently or with disabled people's organisations (DPOs) also known as user-led organisations (ULOs). Many DPO/ULOs offer brokerage services as well as advocacy services.

Sometimes councils have contracts with brokers from DPO/ULOs to do support planning with the service user. Get in touch with your local council or DPO/ULO for the contact details of your local brokerage service.

Find your local DPO
You can find your local DPO/ULO at NHS Choices independent living centre and user led organisations database at:
ⓦ www.nhs.uk/Service-Search/ Support-for-independent-living/ LocationSearch/386

Many of Disability Rights UK's members are disabled people's organisations. You can find a list on our website.

A broker's fees are paid from the direct payments budget if you get your care money from social services.

If you want to use your personal budget to employ a personal assistant (PA) to help you to live independently in your own home or buy care from an agency or do various things during the day, a broker can help you to make the right decision to get the care or other services that best meet your needs.

Using a broker
To manage your support plan a broker can help you to:
- write a support plan based on what you want
- prepare a specific, measurable, attainable, realistic, time-bound (SMART) action plan
- identify indicative costs of implementing the support plan
- manage the personal budget
- plan and manage the right support for you
- write a contingency plan that reflects your personal preferences
- explore solutions to emergency events
- get a more personalised service
- liaise and negotiate with the service providers
- arrange support and care services
- clarify your needs and goals
- identify and apply for various government and non-government funding sources
- identify and access community resources.

To support you with employment administration and management of your personal budget a broker could also:

- recruit, interview and induct staff/PAs
- draft contracts of employment for PAs
- ensure that direct payments funding is used on items approved in the support plan
- help you to keep records of how the budget is being used and spent
- open a separate bank account to access funding
- fill in payroll forms and PAs' timesheets
- liaise with insurance companies and keep a record of insurance certificates
- liaise with payroll/accountants' services
- resolve problems that may arise with the management of your personal budget (as instructed by you and in line with your wishes).

Remember that although a broker can do all of the above, they are acting on your behalf and it is you who decides what you want them to do.

You can find further information on brokerage and training on the website of the National Brokerage Network:
Ⓦ www.nationalbrokeragenetwork.org.uk

For more information
You can find factsheets about self-directed support, support planning, employing a PA and using a broker in the *How we can help* section of the Disability Rights UK website:
Ⓦ www.disabilityrightsuk.org

SUPPORTING FRIENDS AND RELATIVES

If you are providing certain kinds of help for a relative or friend because they have one or more health conditions or disabilities (whether or not you have a condition or disability yourself), you might be considered a 'carer' by the local authority and social security system.

Of course you are still the person's wife, daughter, partner, parent, friend, etc first and this ordinarily requires helping other people out. But if you are providing a lot of support each week, you are entitled to a 'carer's assessment' from your local authority.

Support for 'carers'
People defined as carers can get a range of support. By getting help and by enabling the person you care for to get the support they need, you can make your lives easier and ensure that you have the relationship that you want. For example, if you or your relative gets support to do something they enjoy, this gives the person who does the 'caring' bit a break.

Advice for carers
To find out more about how carers can get support visit the Carers section of NHS choices' website:
Ⓣ www.nhs.uk/CarersDirect

If you need help with your caring role and want to find out about the options available to you, contact the Carers Direct helpline via their online enquiry form or by phone:
Ⓣ 0300 123 1053; textphone 0300 123 1004

Getting the healthcare you need

The NHS is based on the principle that good healthcare should be available to all, regardless of wealth. With the exception of some charges, such as prescriptions and optical and dental services, the NHS is free for anyone who is resident in the UK.

It covers everything from antenatal screening and treatments for long-term conditions, to transplants, emergency treatment, and end-of-life care.

Private healthcare is also available to people who want to and are able to pay for it. Sometimes employers offer private healthcare to their employees.

Your rights

The NHS Constitution
The Constitution is the NHS's ruling document. It gives you important rights including:
- to receive free NHS services without discrimination (except where sanctioned by Parliament)
- to receive local NHS services that are based on local need
- to be treated with a professional standard of care
- to receive drugs and treatments recommended by NICE (National Institute for Health and Clinical Excellence) for use in the NHS and by doctors as appropriate
- for local decisions on funding of other drugs to be made rationally and explained
- to convenient and easy access with clear and transparent decision-making.

Increasingly, primary health care (the GP or health centre) can offer or refer us to a wide range of services in the community that can improve our health and wellbeing – from physiotherapy to counselling – reducing the need to go into hospital, unless it's necessary.

We all need to be advocates for our own health (with support from those we trust) and ask for and get the best and right kind of healthcare. Some of us will have personal health budgets – which give us the power to choose the services and equipment that we need, increasingly at home or locally, rather than in hospital.

PERSONAL HEALTH BUDGETS

Clinical commissioning groups (CCG) in England can now offer adults eligible for NHS continuing care (and children eligible for continuing care) a personal health budget (the amount of money allocated to meet your health and wellbeing needs). The CCG must draw up a care plan with you, setting out your needs and agreeing what the money can be used for.

The budget can be held (as a notional budget) by your NHS team, to buy or provide the agreed services for you. It can be held and managed by a third party (an independent organisation) or you can be given the money as direct payments.

If you choose direct payments, you control and account for the money yourself or your representative or another nominated person manages it on your behalf.

If the patient is under 16, a parent or guardian can manage the money on their behalf.

You don't have to have direct payments, but research shows that people who try them tend to prefer them for the freedom they offer. They feel more in control, and can plan their healthcare to suit their situation and to keep them well, rather than waiting until there is a crisis.

You can use a personal health budget to pay for a wide range of items and services, including therapies, personal care and equipment, as long as they are included in your plan. They cannot be used to pay for GP services, diagnostic tests, screening or immunisation programmes, emergency treatment or NHS prescription charges.

CONTINUING HEALTHCARE

NHS continuing healthcare is a package of care arranged and funded solely by the NHS for people who have complex ongoing healthcare needs (but are not in hospital).

"I've got Raynaud's syndrome in my feet. I've had it since my early thirties, and I also have chronic obstructive pulmonary disease and type 2 diabetes. I manage my long-term health conditions using various person-centred thinking tools and use them to develop the plan for my life. I am now experiencing personalised, responsive and holistic care that not only treats my illnesses, but also suits me and how I want to live my life."

If you are eligible, you can receive NHS continuing healthcare in any setting, for example:

- in your own home – the NHS will pay for healthcare, such as services from a community nurse or specialist therapist, and personal care, such as help with bathing, dressing and laundry
- in a nursing home – as well as healthcare and personal care, the NHS will pay for your nursing home fees, including board and accommodation.

NHS continuing healthcare is free, unlike social and community care services provided by local authorities where you may be charged depending on your income and savings.

INTERMEDIATE CARE

Intermediate Care is a collection of health and social care services aimed at helping people stay in their own home, or care home, instead of going into hospital. It can also help patients to regain their independence after a hospital stay.

The services are provided by teams of professionals that may include nurses, occupational therapists and care assistants. Depending on the person's needs Intermediate Care can be provided for a few days, or several weeks.

RIGHT TO A GP

You have the right to register with a GP if you live within their catchment area. You can choose which GP you want to be registered with.

If a GP refuses to accept you or removes you from their list, they must have reasonable grounds for doing so, and must give you their reasons in writing.

You are still entitled to emergency treatment or for treatment that you get more than once a week until you are accepted by another GP.

Your rights

Accessible information and communication

The Equality Act gives people the right to accessible communication, including in health services.

It's important that people have access to interpretation and other forms of communication support to help them use health services effectively.

The information that you get from health professionals should be easy to understand so that you are clear on anything you need to do.

If you find that you can't make sense of things about your health that are said to you or that are written, you can ask for an explanation or a clearer written version.

You have a right for communication about your health to be in an accessible format. This could be British Sign Language; tactile signing for people who have both a visual and hearing impairment; or sign supported English; or in Easyread format for people with learning disabilities.

If you have difficulty registering with another GP or feel you've been treated unfairly, the NHS England team in your area should find you a GP. For more information visit *NHS services and treatments* in the Common health questions section of NHS Choices:

Ⓦ www.nhs.uk/chq/pages/home.aspx

You are entitled to treatment from a GP at the surgery where you are registered, but you have no automatic right to see your own GP.

A GP must provide any treatment which is immediately necessary in an emergency, even if you are not registered with them.

Problems with registering

Unless the GP's register is full, or you live too far away for home visits, it is unlikely that the GP will refuse to accept you.

"I have hearing difficulties and it is embarrassing when I go to the dentist – I can never hear them when the receptionist calls my name."

You could ask your dental surgery to keep a record of all their patients who are deaf or have hearing loss. Receptionists can then come over and let you know when the dentist is ready to see you, rather than calling out your name. The surgery should agree to this. If they don't agree and they don't have a good reason, they are probably discriminating against you and you should make a complaint.

However, if the GP does refuse to accept you, then they must have reasonable grounds for doing so. These must not have anything to do with age, appearance, disability, gender or gender reassignment, health (including weight), pregnancy or maternity, race, religion, sexual orientation or social class.

Your rights

Your GP must not discriminate against you and must provide 'reasonable adjustments' – changes to how things are done or equipment or interpretation – so that you can access their service.

YOU AND YOUR GP

GPs are often the gateway to health services and more. It is worth finding a GP that you get on with. You don't have to stick with the first person you see or the person you have been used to seeing.

Try to build a good relationship with your GP. Your health is something in which you both have an interest.

Beyond Words produces books, eBooks and other resources for people who find it easier to understand pictures than words. They tell stories that engage and empower people, on themes including health, relationships, death and dying, and crime. As well as a story told in pictures, each Books Beyond Words title has written information, guidelines and resources for readers, families, supporters and professionals.
Ⓦ www.booksbeyondwords.co.uk

Access to medical reports and health records

You have the right to see most health records held about you, subject to certain safeguards. You are entitled to be informed of the uses of the information, who has access to it and how you can arrange to see your records. This information is provided in GP practices and NHS Trusts in the form of posters and leaflets.

For more information on how the information is issued, you may wish to speak to the health professional in charge of your care and support. You may have to pay a fee to see your health records.

You have a right, subject to certain safeguards, to see any medical report written for an employer, prospective employer or insurer, by a medical practitioner who has responsibility for your ongoing care. This could be your GP or consultant and any medical practitioner who has treated you in the past.

Information about your medical history should be kept confidential, and should not be released to people who are not involved in your medical care without your consent. This includes your relatives, unless you are unable to give consent yourself. There are some exceptions to this rule. For example, medical information about you may very occasionally be disclosed if it would prevent serious harm to others.

Medication

If a GP decides you need medication, they will usually give you a prescription. In some cases, for example, if the surgery is in an isolated area, the GP may provide the medication themselves.

A GP must supply any drugs needed for immediate treatment in an emergency. There is no prescription charge for these.

The Choice and Medication website provides information about medications used in mental health settings to help people make informed decisions.

W www.cmhp.org.uk/about-cmhp/choice-and-medication

Getting medication right

If you have been prescribed medication you should have been given an information leaflet describing why you have been prescribed it, any side effects and what you can do to make it work effectively.

Many NHS trusts run medicines management teams to provide clear, accessible information about medicines. They have a medicines information helpline for any questions or concerns about medication. Your local pharmacy can also be a good source of advice.

Second opinions

You can ask your GP to arrange a second opinion either from a specialist or another GP. However, the GP does not have to do this if they do not think it necessary. You have no right to a second opinion, although a health professional will rarely refuse one.

You do have the right to see a GP competent to deal with your particular case. If a GP refers you for a second opinion, you cannot insist on seeing a particular practitioner. However, you should not be referred to someone you do not wish to see.

If a GP is unsure about a diagnosis, they could be found negligent if they fail to refer you to a specialist and you suffered as a result of this. If you have not been referred for a second opinion and have suffered as a consequence, you may wish to complain.

The NHS Health Check programme
This programme aims to help prevent heart disease, stroke, diabetes, kidney disease and certain types of dementia. Health checks are available for adults in England aged 40 to 74 (without a pre-existing condition). There are also annual health checks for people with long-term mental health problems and for adults with learning disabilities.

Read more about healthchecks:
W www.healthcheck.nhs.uk

NHS Choices
NHS Choices is an online resource with information about conditions, treatments, local services and healthy living. It is designed to help you find, choose and compare health services in England and to put you in control of your healthcare.
W www.nhs.uk/Pages/HomePage.aspx

RIGHT TO HOSPITAL TREATMENT

You cannot receive NHS hospital treatment without being referred by your GP, unless you are attending a special clinic, for example, for the treatment of sexually transmitted diseases, or you need urgent medical attention in an emergency.

Hospital choice

If you are referred for a first outpatient hospital appointment, you can choose to go to any NHS hospital that provides a service or a private hospital. To find out more about choosing your hospital, visit:
Ⓦ www.nhs.uk

TREATMENT WHICH MAY NOT BE AVAILABLE ON THE NHS

Access to some forms of treatment, for example, in-vitro fertilisation, may be subject to local health priorities. Some treatment may not be provided in your area. Access may depend on your need.

An NHS clinic has refused fertility services to us, because we are a deaf lesbian couple. Can they do this?

No, they can't. If they refuse to treat you either because you are a lesbian couple when the treatment would be offered to a straight couple, or deaf and it would be offered to a hearing couple, this is discrimination. It's against the law. You will need to get advice about how to take this further. However, if they don't offer the treatment to any couples, regardless of sexual orientation or disability, you won't be able to complain about discrimination.

However, the NHS Constitution says that local decisions about the funding of drugs and treatment must be made rationally, following proper consideration of the evidence. Information about local decisions must be made readily available to the public.

Your rights

The NHS and private healthcare providers must not discriminate against you because of age, disability, gender or gender reassignment, pregnancy or maternity, race, religion or belief and sexual orientation when they decide what treatment to give you as a patient.

SEEING A CONSULTANT

You have the right to choose a particular team, headed by a named consultant for your first outpatient appointment, provided that the doctor referring you agrees that your choice is clinically appropriate.

You can choose a team based at any hospital. However, you don't have the right to choose a particular consultant-led team for certain services, including accident and emergency, maternity and cancer care and treatment.

You may wish to get a second opinion after seeing a consultant, either as an out-patient or an in-patient. You will need to request this from the consultant, who may arrange for you to see someone else. If the consultant does not agree, you could ask your GP to help.

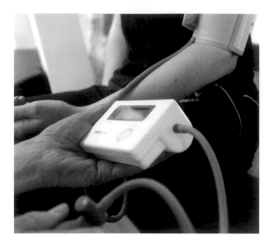

CARE IN HOSPITAL
Choosing a hospital
You have the right to choose from any hospital when your GP refers you to see a specialist for further treatment. Your GP should discuss this with you.

Booking an appointment
The Choose and Book system enables you to make your first outpatient appointment at a hospital or clinic at a convenient time for you, online or by phone. You may be able to choose a hospital according to what matters most to you, whether it's location, waiting times, reputation or clinical performance.

📞 0845 608 8888
🌐 www.chooseandbook.nhs.uk

Having used the Choose and Book system, Sarah Payne commented: "All the information I would want to base my decision on is displayed on the Choose and Book screen in front of me. It showed me locations, dates, times, waiting times and types of clinic; it made booking my appointment effortless."

You can book the appointment yourself. Your GP must give you an appointment request slip first. This must have a reference number and password which you use when you make your booking.

Hospital waiting lists
You may be unable to get the hospital treatment you need immediately, and may have to go on a waiting list. Waiting lists do not operate on a first-come, first-served basis. Where you are on a waiting list depends on a range of circumstances and may change. If your condition deteriorates dramatically, your GP may recommend you be seen as a matter of greater urgency. How long you will have to wait for a date to see a specialist or have an operation, will therefore depend on the severity of your condition, how busy the specialist is and other demands on the hospital facilities.

If you are waiting to be admitted to hospital, you should contact the hospital appointments' department or the consultant on a regular basis, reminding the hospital staff that you are still waiting. If you are prepared to go into hospital at short notice you should say so, in case a cancellation occurs. Keep your GP informed of your condition, particularly if it deteriorates.

Your rights

Under the NHS Constitution, you have the right to use services within maximum waiting times. If this is not possible, your local healthcare commissioner must try to offer you suitable alternative treatment providers if you ask it to do so.

Waiting times

If you go into an accident and emergency department (A&E), you should be assessed immediately. Staff should always try to make sure you do not wait more than four hours between attending A&E and admission, treatment or discharge.

NHS 111: Emergency or urgent care

If you have a health problem that is urgent but not life-threatening, call the NHS 111 service. Trained health advisers will asses your symptoms, advise on self-treatment or refer you to a local service that can help you. Calls are free from landlines and mobiles and the service operates 24-hours a day, 365 days a year.

T 111

Operation cancellations

If your operation is cancelled, you should be offered an alternative date.

If your operation is cancelled for non-medical reasons on or after the day you are admitted to hospital, you should be offered another treatment date within 28 days. If this is not possible, your treatment should be funded at the time and at the hospital of your choice.

STANDARDS OF CARE

The Care Quality Commission (CQC) is the independent regulator of health and social care in England. It checks all hospitals in England to see if they are meeting government standards.

You can find out about what to expect from your local hospital by checking the inspection reports on their website.

The CQC cannot deal with individual complaints but you can give them feedback about the standard of care you received, to share your experiences, (whether good or bad) by phone, email or online.

The Care Quality Commission

CQC National Customer Service Centre, Citygate, Gallo gate, Newcastle upon Tyne NE1 4PA

T 03000 61 61 61
E enquiries@cqc.org.uk
W www.cqc.org.uk

The Regulation and Quality Improvement Authority is Northern Ireland's independent health and social care regulator.

T 028 9051 7500
E info@rqia.org.uk
W www.rqia.org.uk

Healthcare Improvement Scotland's role is to improve the care of patients and to regulate independent healthcare services through an inspection framework.

T 0131 623 4300
E comments.his@nhs.net
W www.healthcareimprovement scotland.org

The Care and Social Services Inspectorate Wales is responsible for inspecting social care and social services in Wales to make sure that they are safe for the people who use them.

T 0300 7900 126
E cssiw@wales.gsi.gov.uk
W http://cssiw.org.uk

CONSENT

Examination and treatment

You should not be examined, operated on or given any treatment without your consent, unless:

- you have a notifiable infectious disease or are a carrier of a notifiable disease
- you have been detained under the Mental Health Act, in certain limited circumstances
- your life is in danger, you are unconscious and you cannot indicate your wishes
- the patient is a child who is a ward of court and the court decides that a specific treatment is in the child's interests
- a court or someone who has parental responsibility authorises treatment. A person whose treatment is authorised by a court must be given an opportunity to defend their case against treatment in court.

In some cases, it is good practice to ask you, the patient, to sign a consent form, but in other cases consent can be obtained orally.

For example, it is good practice to obtain written consent for any procedure or treatment carrying substantial risk or side effects. If you are capable, it is good practice to obtain written consent for general anaesthesia, surgery and certain forms of drug therapy. Oral or written consent should be recorded in your notes with relevant details of health professionals' explanations. If you need any interpretation or other assistance to help you to discuss or consent to treatment, this must be provided.

Even if you sign a consent form, the signature may not be a valid form of consent if you have not been given appropriate information to be able to give informed consent. Similarly, consent for one procedure does not imply consent for a further procedure or form of treatment.

The doctor must inform you of the nature, consequences, and any substantial risks involved in the treatment or operation, before you give your consent. It is for the doctor to decide exactly how much to tell you. You can change your mind at any time, right up to the operating theatre.

Capacity to consent to treatment

There may be situations where there are questions about whether you have capacity to consent to treatment. A person lacks capacity if their brain or mind is impaired and they do not have the ability to use and understand information to make a decision at the time on the specific issue. Examples could include dementia, brain damage, or intoxication through drugs or alcohol misuse.

Doctors and other staff are required by law to assume first that you are capable (many people with dementia, for instance, are able to make decisions with the right support and encouragement). They must then offer any support that may help you to make a decision (for instance, putting the information into a format that you understand, or involving an advocate to help you express your decision).

They can only judge capacity in relation to a particular decision – they cannot generalise and say that because you don't understand all the implications of a particular operation that means you aren't capable of deciding where you want to live, for instance. A 'capacity assessment' should be carried out by a health professional. If it is felt that you do not have capacity for the particular decision, they will need to carefully consider what is in your 'best interests', bearing in mind anything you have said before and the views of those close to you, before making a decision. Your wishes should always be taken into account to the greatest extent possible.

Right to refuse treatment

You can refuse any treatment if you wish, if you have the capacity to do so. When you visit a doctor, this usually implies consent to examination and treatment. The doctor cannot act against specific instructions, so you should tell the doctor about any treatment you do not want.

If there are alternative treatments which can be used to treat your condition, you should be given information on these and have the chance to discuss options with your doctor.

Forcing treatment on you against your will is assault.

If you have a mental health condition and are detained under mental health law, you may be required to take psychiatric medication even if you do have capacity; but not to accept surgery or physical treatment.

Treatment for a child

If a parent, guardian or child refuse to give consent for treatment which a doctor thinks is necessary, the doctor is still obliged to treat the child. However, if the child has capacity for decision-making in this instance, the doctors also have an obligation to explain the options and to seek the views of the child.

The actions the doctor takes will depend on how urgently the treatment is needed. When a child's life is in danger, the doctor has the right to do whatever is needed to save the child's life. If a parent or guardian either fail to provide medical help for a child, or unreasonably refuse to allow treatment, they can be prosecuted for neglect.

LIFE-SUSTAINING TREATMENT

Life-sustaining treatment is treatment that replaces or supports ailing bodily functions. For example, a mechanical ventilator can help you to breathe, or taking antibiotics can help your body fight infection.

You may find it helpful to talk to a doctor or nurse about the kinds of treatments you might be offered in the future, and what it might mean if you choose to have or not have them.

Many people with health conditions and disabilities feel anxious when in hospital about perceptions of their quality of life. You may feel reassured if you or a relative states clearly that you do or you don't want life-sustaining treatment in the case of a crisis. It lets your family and health professionals know whether you want to have treatment or refuse specific treatments in the future. This is so that they know your wishes if you are unable to communicate.

An advance directive is a decision you can make now to say what kinds of treatment you would want in particular circumstances – including hydration and nutrition – and whether you want to refuse a specific type of treatment at some time in the future. Although saying what you do want won't be binding on doctors it is something that they have to take account of.

The treatments you are deciding to refuse or specifying that you would want in particular circumstances must all be named in the advance decision.

You can specify that you do want life-saving treatment, including hydration and nutrition. If you wish to refuse life-sustaining treatments in circumstances where you might die as a result, you need to state this clearly. Life-sustaining treatment is sometimes called life-saving treatment.

You may want to refuse a treatment in some situations but not others. If this is the case, you need to be clear about all the circumstances in which you want to refuse this treatment.

You can refuse a treatment that could potentially keep you alive. This includes ventilation and cardio pulmonary resuscitation (CPR) which may be used if you cannot breathe by yourself or if your heart stops. You may want to discuss this with a doctor or nurse who knows about your medical history before you make up your mind.

A 'do not resuscitate' (DNR) order is a legal order written either in the hospital or on a legal form. The idea is to respect the wishes of a patient not to undergo CPR if their heart was to stop or they were to stop breathing. The reasoning is that such treatment can be traumatic and is not always successful. Research shows that only about 5% of patients who require CPR outside the hospital and only 15% of patients who require CPR while in the hospital survive. Some people feel that not resuscitating a person can allow a 'natural death'.

Occasionally, people with disabilities or health conditions have had DNR notices put on their medical notes without their consent. If you or a relative is seriously ill and in hospital, you may want to make clear your wishes about resuscitation, whether or not you are asked about it.

Any wishes in this area that are made explicit should be as detailed as possible and reviewed regularly. For example, you might decide because you have young children that you would like everything done to keep you alive in the case of catastrophic injury. You might or might not make a different decision in your 90s about the level of active intervention that you would want.

Your rights

Knowing your rights will help you get the best from the NHS and social care services. Often knowing your rights can help – without actually having to use them. For instance, you can say which hospital you want to go to and mention that you understand you have a right to choose.

If you feel you are being unjustly treated in breach of your rights, you may want to take action. You can do this by telling someone you trust, seeking help from an advocacy service, or contacting the complaints team of the service.

There are also outside bodies that you can complain to and organisations can help you access your rights.
- Ⓦ www.nhs.uk/CarersDirect/yourself/ help-for-you/Pages/Advocacy.aspx

THE NHS CONSTITUTION

The NHS Constitution sets out your rights as a patient. It outlines NHS commitments to patients and staff, and 'the responsibilities that the public, patients and staff owe to one another to ensure that the NHS operates fairly and effectively'. NHS bodies and private and third sector providers supplying NHS services are required to take account of the constitution in their decisions and actions.

To download the NHS Constitution and read more about what you can expect from the health service, visit:
- Ⓦ www.nhs.uk/choiceintheNHS/ Rightsandpledges

What you have a right to expect:
- If your GP refers you for treatment, you should be able to start your consultant-led treatment within a maximum of 18 weeks from referral for non-urgent conditions. Where cancer is suspected, you should be seen by a cancer specialist within a maximum of two weeks. If this is not possible, the NHS has to take all reasonable steps to offer you a range of alternatives.
- If your GP refers you to see a consultant you may have the choice of a number of hospitals. You might want to choose a hospital that has better results for your treatment than others, or one near your place of work. Ask your GP for more information.
- You can view your personal health records and have any factual inaccuracies corrected. You don't have to give a reason to see them, just ask at your GP surgery and make an appointment to come in.
- If you are unhappy with a NHS service and decide to make a complaint, you have the right to have that complaint acknowledged by the organisation receiving the complaint within three working days (excluding weekends and bank holidays). You also have the right for that complaint to be investigated properly.

NHS pledges

The chart on the following pages describes patient and public rights and sets out how the NHS pledges go beyond the legal minimum in each area

	People's rights	NHS pledges
Access to health services	• Receive free NHS services (except where sanctioned by Parliament) without discrimination • Local NHS services that are based on local need • In certain circumstances, treatment in other European Economic Area countries	• Provision of convenient and easy access • Clear and transparent decision-making • Smooth transition between NHS services
Quality of care and the environment	• To be treated with a professional standard of care • To be treated by appropriately qualified and experienced staff in a properly approved organisation that meets required levels of safety and quality • To expect NHS organisations to monitor and make efforts to improve their quality of care	• Services provided in a clean and safe environment that is fit for purpose, in line with national best practice • Continuous improvement in the quality of services • Identification and sharing of best practice in quality of care and treatments
Nationally approved treatments and programmes	• Drugs and treatments recommended by NICE for use in the NHS and by doctors as appropriate • Local decisions on funding of other drugs made rationally and explained • Vaccinations recommended for national programmes by the Joint Committee on Vaccination and Immunisation	• Screening programmes as recommended by the UK National Screening Committee
Respect, consent and confidentiality	• To be treated with dignity and respect • Accept or refuse treatment or physical examination • You can expect to be given information about recommended treatment, risks and alternative treatment available • You can expect the NHS to keep your confidential information safe and secure • You can access your own health records which will be used to manage your treatment	• To share with you any letters sent between clinicians about your care

From The NHS Constitution staff guide (Department of Health, 2009)

	People's rights	NHS pledges
Informed choice	• Choice of GP practice • To be accepted by that practice, unless there are reasonable grounds for refusal • To be informed of any reason for refusal • To express a preference for a doctor within a practice and for the practice to try to comply • To make choices about their care – options will change over time • Information to help them make choices about care	• To inform patients about healthcare services available to them nationally and locally • To provide easily accessible, reliable and relevant information to help people make choices, including information on the quality of clinical services, where robust information is available
Involvement in healthcare and the NHS	• Involvement in discussions and decisions about their healthcare • Information to help them to be involved in discussions and decisions • Involvement (directly or through representatives) in planning healthcare services • Involvement in proposals for changes to services and the way services are operated	• Provision of convenient and easy access • Clear and transparent decision-making • Smooth transition between NHS services
Complaint and redress	• Complaints to be dealt with efficiently and properly investigated • To know the outcome of complaints • To go to the Health Service Ombudsman, if they are not happy with the way their complaint is handled • A claim for judicial review, if they think they have been directly affected by an unlawful NHS decision or action • Compensation, where they have been harmed by negligent treatment	• To treat patients and the public with courtesy • To provide appropriate support throughout the handling of a complaint • Not to allow a complaint to adversely affect future treatment • To acknowledge mistakes when they happen, to apologise, explain what went wrong and to put things right quickly and effectively • To learn from complaints and claims, and to use lessons to improve NHS services

THE EQUALITY ACT AND THE NHS

The Equality Act 2010 means that the NHS must try to remove discrimination and reduce inequalities in care.

Whenever you need healthcare, medical treatment or social care, you have the right to be treated fairly and not to be discriminated against, regardless of your 'protected characteristics'. The Equality Act sets out that every person should be treated as an individual and with respect and dignity.

The laws mean that all NHS organisations will be required to make sure health and social care services are fair and meet the needs of everyone, whatever their background or circumstances.

The Equality Act 2010 offers protection to nine characteristics:
- age
- race
- sex
- gender reassignment status
- disability
- religion or belief
- sexual orientation
- marriage and civil partnership status
- pregnancy and maternity.

The law also protects people who are at risk of discrimination by association or perception. This could include, for example, someone who provides support to a person with a health condition or disability.

Health and social care services covered by the laws under the Equality Act 2010 include:

- all NHS providers (eg hospitals)
- all NHS commissioners (eg GP practices)
- those supporting older and disabled people in their homes
- care in day centres, residential or nursing homes
- those caring for children who don't live with their parents.

It doesn't matter whether the service is provided by a public authority or an independent provider.

The Equality and Human Rights Commission has developed guidance for users of health and social care. You can find it in the *Private and public sector guidance* section of their website:
Ⓦ www.equalityhumanrights.com

THE CARE ACT 2014

The Care Act places a duty on local authorities in England to provide or arrange services that reduce needs for support among people and their carers in the local area and/or contribute towards preventing or delaying the development of such needs.

Preventive services should operate at three levels:
1 Primary prevention to stop care and support needs from developing among those who do not have them, for example through health promotion or action to reduce isolation.
2 Secondary prevention, for people at increased risk of developing needs, which could involve housing adaptations or telecare that prevent deterioration.

3   Tertiary prevention for people with established needs to help improve independence, for example through reablement.

Assessments should seek to promote independence and resilience by identifying people's strengths and informal support networks, as well as their needs and the risks they may face, and asking what a good life means to them and how they think it can be achieved in partnership with professionals.

Section 4 of the Act places a duty on councils to establish and maintain a service providing information and advice to local people on care and support.

Sections 9-13 sets out the Act's provisions on assessing adults and carers, including duties to assess adults if they appear to have needs for care and support, and carers if they appear to have needs for support. These are fleshed out in the draft statutory guidance.

If a council thinks a person may lack capacity to make a decision or plan, even after being offered support, then a social worker or other suitably qualified professional needs to assess their capacity in relation to the decision being made (for example whether the person has the capacity to decide whether family members should be involved in their care planning).

In line with the Mental Capacity Act (MCA), care and support plans must minimise planned restrictions and restraints on the person as much as possible.

These planned restrictions and restraints must be documented and reported to a social worker to agree. Significant restraints and restrictions that amount to a deprivation of liberty must be authorised under the Deprivation of Liberty Safeguards (Dols). But the guidance says that in most cases a deprivation of liberty would be avoided with proper person-centred planning.

During the planning process the individual and their social worker, or another professional, may have recorded a date for review of the plan. The guidance says this can help to personalise care and support and assist councils in planning their workloads. But the authority should still keep the plan under review outside these dates.

Social workers will often be the most appropriate professionals to carry out assessments of young people with complex needs who are making the transition to adult services. The guidance says transition assessments should be carried out early enough to ensure that the right care and support is in place when the young person moves to adult care and support.

A RIGHT TO ADVOCACY

Councils have a duty to provide people with an independent advocate during assessment and support planning if they would otherwise have difficulty in understanding or communicating information, and have no one else to represent them. Advocates are also available for accessing health and other services.

THE HUMAN RIGHTS ACT

Under UK law, you should be looked after and treated fairly and with dignity whenever you are given health or social care services. This applies to everyone, regardless of where they are given care and who does the caring. This is part of the UK Human Rights Act.

Several rights may apply because of this law, including the right to:
- life
- liberty
- respect for private and family life, home and correspondence
- not be tortured or treated in an inhuman or degrading way.

Other laws may also protect you from discrimination because of who you are, including some protection for carers under the rules designed to protect people with health conditions or disabilities.

For example, if you are an older person, this should not stop you from having treatment similar to that which a younger person would be given. Your right to a private and family life should mean that you don't have to live somewhere different against your will because of a health condition. For example you should not have to be separated from your partner.

MENTAL CAPACITY ACT

If you have a condition such as dementia or a learning disability, or you have had a severe head injury, various Mental Capacity Acts can protect your right to make your own decisions wherever possible.

The Acts also say that when you need help, the people helping you must involve you as much as possible and protect your rights.

The key principle of the Mental Capacity Acts is that you are presumed to have the capacity to make all your own decisions.

You also have rights known as Deprivation of Liberty Safeguards. These are a part of the Mental Capacity Acts that protect your rights if you are unable to care for yourself or keep yourself safe, and it may be best for you to have some restrictions on your liberty. They ensure that any restrictions are lawful and that the least restrictive options are applied.

In England and Wales
The relevant legislation is the Mental Capacity Act 2005:
- Ⓦ www.legislation.gov.uk/ ukpga/2005/9/contents

In Northern Ireland
Decision-making is governed by the common law. The Northern Ireland Assembly is working towards new law to cover both supporting people's legal capacity and a new approach to people with mental health problems, bringing the two areas of law together to make it fairer for everyone.

In Scotland
The relevant legislation is the Adults with Incapacity (Scotland) Act 2000:
- Ⓦ www.legislation.gov.uk/asp/2000/4/ contents

UNITED NATIONS CONVENTION ON THE RIGHTS OF PERSONS WITH DISABILITIES

Article 25 of the UNCRPD says:

- Disabled people have the right to enjoy the best possible health.
- Disabled people have the right to the same range, quality and standard of free and affordable healthcare as everyone else – including sexual health and fertility services.
- Governments should ensure healthcare professionals are trained to provide an equal service, on a human rights basis. This includes making sure that disabled people have access to information about treatment so that they know what treatment they are agreeing to.
- Governments should provide the health services and treatment disabled people need for their specific impairments, including services that help people regain their independence after they have developed an impairment. They should ensure impairments and health conditions are identified early and that people get early support. These services need to be close to where people live – including in rural areas.
- Governments should take steps to make sure health and life insurance policies do not discriminate against disabled people.

Article 19 of the UNCRPD says:

- Disabled people have an equal right to live in and take part in the community.
- Disabled people have the right to the same choice and control as non-disabled people.

- Governments should do everything they can to ensure disabled people enjoy these rights.

And that Governments should ensure that:

- disabled people have the right to choose where they live and who they live with – no disabled person should be unlawfully forced into a particular living arrangement (for example be forced to live in a care home against their will)
- disabled people have access to a wide range of support services (at home and in the community) including personal assistance to prevent isolation and support inclusion
- disabled people can access the same community services as everyone else.

Using the Convention

A deaf couple want to access fertility treatment because of unexplained infertility. Their GP tells them that they are not eligible because they have an inheritable condition. They are able to challenge this by referencing the Equality Act and their Convention rights.

RIGHTS FOR FAMILY AND FRIENDS

If you provide unpaid support to someone close to you – helping them with domestic tasks, such as cleaning, shopping and bills, cooking for them or helping them with washing and dressing, for example – you have rights and you may be entitled to social security payments.

You may be referred to as a 'carer' in your interactions with public authorities.

As a carer, you have specific legal rights and entitlements. Knowing your rights can help you to get the support that you need.

These rights for carers include:
- the right to have your needs assessed by your local authority
- the right to receive direct payments so that you can chose what services to have
- rights in the workplace.

Sharon Coleman's son Oliver was born with a rare condition affecting his breathing and he also has a hearing impairment.

Sharon brought a case claiming she was forced to resign from her job as a legal secretary after being harassed by her employers and being refused flexible working, which other employees were granted. Her case was that she was targeted because she has a child with a disability, and was denied flexible work arrangements offered to her colleagues without disabled children.

Sharon's victory before the European Court of Justice clarified that UK disability discrimination law provides protection on the grounds of someone's association (including caring responsibilities) with a disabled person. The Equality Act 2010 further clarified this position.

Anyone aged 16 or above, who provides a 'regular and substantial amount of care' for someone aged 18 or over, has the right to an assessment of their needs.

The local authority also has a responsibility to make sure a young carer's own wellbeing is looked after and that they receive the necessary support. So, a 16 or 17 year old who cares for someone, even for a limited period, may be entitled to an assessment.

Carers and employment rights

Working parents of disabled children under 18 and people supporting an adult relative living at the same address both have the right to request flexible working arrangements.

While you have the right to ask for flexible work in these circumstances, it is important to know that employers are not bound to grant these requests. However, they must give business reasons if they refuse.

Carers also have the right to take unpaid time off work for dependants (the people they care for/support) in an emergency.

Your rights

People are protected under the Equality Act 2010 on grounds of association with someone who is disabled. So if, for example, you feel you have been discriminated against at work because you are supporting a disabled child or adult, you have a right of redress.

MENTAL HEALTH LEGISLATION

Mental health conditions, including anxiety, depression, bipolar and schizophrenia, affect up to one in four people every year. Anxiety and depression are extremely common. In 2010-11 over 1.25 million adults accessed NHS services for severe or enduring mental health problems.

The Mental Health Acts of 1983 and 2007 set out various legal rights that apply to people with severe mental health conditions in England and Wales. They also contain the powers that, in extreme cases, allow some people with mental health problems to be compulsorily detained in a psychiatric hospital.

Health, disability and risk

'Health and safety' is, on occasions, used as a false excuse to justify discriminating against people with health conditions and disabilities.

When accessing health or social care services you may have to be robust in responding to suggestions or directions that take a very risk averse approach.

This can happen in a variety of situations, for example if you are told it would be safer to go into a residential home – but you want to have the right support to stay at home; or if you have a health condition or disability and want to become, or are, pregnant.

Some people can find themselves viewed through the lens of 'risk'.

In the majority of cases, people are admitted to psychiatric hospital on a voluntary basis. They have exactly the same rights as anyone going into hospital for any treatment, and they can leave whenever they want.

In other cases, people can be detained in a psychiatric hospital for certain periods of time. For example, the Mental Health Act 1983 authorises people to be detained for assessment or treatment.

When a person is compulsorily detained in hospital, it's sometimes referred to as being 'sectioned'. The decision to detain an individual is made under a particular section of the Mental Health Act 1983.

This can particularly include those with learning disabilities, autistic spectrum/ neurodiversity conditions and mental health conditions.

People with mental health conditions in particular are viewed as a risk to themselves or other people – which can lead to knee-jerk decisions to detain people in hospital, rather than working together on the best solution.

Good practice from the Royal College of Psychiatrists says you should be involved in any risk assessment and be able to come up with a plan to manage risk that works for you.

For instance, you may know your own triggers to becoming unwell – and be able to make a plan to get the right support at those times to prevent a crisis.

Section 2 of the Mental Health Act allows a person to be detained for a maximum period of 28 days so they can be assessed.

Section 3 allows a person to be detained so they can receive treatment. The maximum period of detention in this case is six months, but more time may be authorised.

The law states that when someone is detained in hospital for a long period of time, it must be shown that medical treatment appropriate to the individual's mental health condition is available.

Research shows that detaining people under the Mental Health Act is not always appropriate or effective. It can be a way of managing people rather than supporting them – for example, young black men are many times more likely to be detained than other groups.

Around the UK
The Mental Health Acts of 1983 and 2007 apply in England and Wales.

In Northern Ireland, the Mental Health (Northern Ireland) Order 1986 covers the assessment, treatment and rights of people with a mental health condition:
- ⓦ www.nidirect.gov.uk/the-mental-health-act

In Scotland, the equivalent act is the Mental Health (Care and Treatment) (Scotland Act) 2003:
- ⓦ www.legislation.gov.uk/asp/2003/13/contents

Understanding sectioning
The Mental Health Act in England and Wales is the law which sets out when you can be admitted, detained and treated against your wishes. It is also known as being 'sectioned' as you are detained under a 'section' (paragraph) of the Act.

For this to happen, certain people must agree that you have a mental disorder that requires a stay in hospital. There you will have an assessment and be given treatment if needed. In theory, this is only done when you are putting your own safety or someone else's at risk or in the interests of your health. In practice, while it may sometimes be appropriate, it is also sometimes used unnecessarily.

Why could you get sectioned?
To be sectioned, you are supposed to have a mental health condition that needs urgent assessment or treatment.

How long will I get sectioned for?
The two most common 'sections' of the Mental Health Act are section 2, which means you can be detained for observation for 28 days, and section 3, which means you can be held for a maximum of six months. This can be extended if doctors think you're still unwell and need further treatment.

"After three months, if you still don't want to have treatment, or are not able to make the decision, a Second Opinion Appointed Doctor will come and see you," says Dr Tony Zigmond from the Royal College of Psychiatrists. "This doctor is independent of your hospital doctor and will decide what medication you need and whether the treatment the hospital wishes to provide can be given to you."

Can I leave hospital if I've been sectioned?

Not if you've been sectioned under sections 2 and 3 of the Mental Health Act. You can leave temporarily, but only with the permission of your hospital doctor. They'll tell you how long you can be away for, where you can go, and whether you'll need someone with you. When you're sectioned under a community treatment order, you can be admitted to hospital if you don't follow the care plan agreed with your doctor.

I want to leave – what can I do?

Under sections 2 and 3 you have a right to appeal to the Mental Health Review Tribunal. This is an independent body. The tribunal will read reports written by members of your care team and hear your views. At the end of the tribunal, they'll decide if your sectioning order should end or continue. You can also appeal to the hospital managers.

How can I get myself sectioned?

Usually, sectioning is something that happens against your will because you don't think you need help. If you feel really desperate you don't have to get sectioned to get help.

"If a young person is feeling ill and in despair what they want is help," says Dr Zigmond. "The legal principle if you want to go into hospital is that this should be arranged voluntarily with your consent. Being sectioned is for people who do not wish to go into hospital, not for those that do. If you recognise you need help, you will be willing to accept treatment."

How can I get un-sectioned?

Doctors will discharge you when they feel you are ready. A family member or your partner can also ask for you to be discharged. Once they've requested this, doctors have up to 72 hours to assess whether it's safe for you to leave hospital. If you don't agree with the decision, you can apply to a Mental Health Review Tribunal see:

Ⓦ www.gov.uk/mental-health-tribunal/overview

I'm worried about my own or someone else's mental health – if I ask for support, will I/they be sectioned?

Contact your local social services. They can arrange a mental health needs assessment and provide access to support. "A family member can go to their local social services and ask for an assessment of the person they wish to become a patient," says Dr Zigmond. "However, it's only when a person requires significant help and is refusing this that a sectioning order under the Mental Health Act would be considered."

Taking away someone's liberty is an infringement of their human rights. While it might occasionally be justified when someone is in extreme crisis, it should be used very rarely and for the shortest periods possible. The Care Quality Commission (the inspector) has said that there should not be a culture of coercion in mental health services.

Rethink is a national mental health charity that provides advice and information to anyone affected by mental health problems. To read more about mental health laws visit the *Living with mental illness* section of Rethink's website:
- Ⓦ www.rethink.org/living-with-mental-illness

Community treatment orders

If you have been in hospital under the Mental Health Act, a clinician (usually your psychiatrist) can arrange for you to have a community treatment order CTO). This means that instead of discharging you completely, you have supervised treatment when you leave hospital.

For more information
To find out more about community treatment orders:
- Ⓦ www.rethink.org/living-with-mental-illness/mental-health-laws/community-treatment-orders

You have to follow certain conditions if you are on a community treatment order. These conditions are designed to ensure that you continue your treatment and to protect you from harming

yourself or other people. If you break a condition or your clinician' feels you have become unwell again, you can be made to return to hospital.

When things go wrong

Sometimes, things go wrong. You may find that:
- you disagree with a decision about your health or social care needs
- you disagree with the outcome of a consultation or assessment
- you believe standards or quality of care have been poor
- you believe the treatment or amount of care you have been allocated has not been enough
- you believe the costs of care are unfair
- you feel that staff have behaved badly or inappropriately.

HOW TO COMPLAIN ABOUT THE SERVICE YOU ARE RECEIVING

You can clear up a lot of problems by having an informal chat with a member of staff or the manager of a service.

If this does not resolve the issue, you may want to make a more formal complaint.

For more information
For details of the procedure to make a complaint about hospitals, GP practices and other NHS services:
- Ⓦ www.nhs.uk/choiceintheNHS/Rightsandpledges/complaints

For details of how to make a complaint about social care services:
- Ⓦ www.lgo.org.uk/adult-social-care

TO COMPLAIN ABOUT A DECISION MADE BY A HEALTHCARE PROVIDER

If you have a complaint about an NHS organisation, make it as soon as you can. Complaining directly might get the matter resolved quickly. Explain why you're unhappy and how you want them to put things right.

If you would like help with making a complaint, you can ask your local Healthwatch (in England) to put you in touch with the NHS complaints advocacy provider for your area.

Healthwatch
☎ 03000 683 000
🌐 www.healthwatch.co.uk
Healthwatch England is the national consumer champion in health and care. It has statutory powers to ensure the voice of the consumer is strengthened and heard by those who commission, deliver and regulate health and care services.

You can get involved in its inquiries and other work to help improve healthcare in your area or nationally.

Healthwatch provides guides to help people make complaints about health and social care services:
🌐 www.healthwatch.co.uk/complaints/guides

Healthwatch also looks for patterns in concerns raised and where necessary raises them with local services or national bodies to try to put things right.

Give the NHS a chance to resolve your complaint and give you their final response before taking things further. Make sure you keep copies of all letters about your complaint.

Around the UK
In Northern Ireland, you can contact the Patient and Client Council who can provide free and confidential advice, information and help to make a complaint. Specialist advocacy services may also be available. Complaints managers or the Patient and Client Council can tell you about these.
🌐 www.patientclientcouncil.hscni.net

In Scotland, NHS Services Scotland can direct you to your particular health board to make a complaint.
🌐 www.nhsnss.org/pages/contact/feedback_and_complaints.php

In Wales you can get help from your local community health council.
🌐 www.communityhealthcouncils.org.uk

Taking a complaint to the Ombudsman

If you're unhappy with how the NHS has dealt with your complaint, contact the Parliamentary and Health Service Ombudsman, which considers complaints about government departments and agencies in the UK and the NHS in England.

Its role is to investigate complaints that individuals have been treated unfairly or have received poor service from government departments and other public organisations and the NHS in England.
Ⓦ www.ombudsman.org.uk

Around the UK

In Northern Ireland it is the Northern Ireland Commissioner for Complaints (the Ombudsman).
Ⓦ www.ni-ombudsman.org.uk

In Scotland it is the Scottish Public Services Ombudsman.
Ⓦ www.spso.org.uk

In Wales it is the Public Services Ombudsman for Wales.
Ⓦ www.ombudsman-wales.org.uk

PROBLEMS WITH HEALTH, SOCIAL CARE AND GP PRACTICES

The Care Quality Commission (CQC) is the independent health and adult social care regulator for England. It makes sure that health and social care services provide people with safe, effective, compassionate, high-quality services and encourages them to improve. It publishes what it finds, including performance ratings to help people choose care.

CQC National Customer Service Centre
Ⓣ 03000 616161
Ⓦ www.cqc.org.uk

TO COMPLAIN ABOUT A DECISION MADE BY THE LOCAL AUTHORITY?

Your council must have a clear reason for deciding:

- not to give you an assessment
- not to give you a direct payment or personal budget
- not to place you in the residential care home you prefer if this is what you want.

They must tell you what decision they have made and why.

Your council will have its own complaints procedure and be able to tell you how to make a complaint. Should you wish to do so, you can complain to your council about their decision. Every council must publish their procedures for dealing with complaints.

If you exhaust your local council's complaints procedure, you could take your issue to the relevant Ombudsman:

Local Government Ombudsman (England)
- ☏ 0300 061 0614
- ⓦ www.lgo.org.uk

Scottish Public Services Ombudsman
- ☏ 0800 377 7330
- ⓦ www.spso.org.uk

Public Service Ombudsman for Wales
- ☏ 0845 601 0987
- ⓦ www.ombudsman-wales.org.uk

Northern Ireland Ombudsman
- ☏ 0800 34 3424
- ⓦ www.ni-ombudsman.org.uk

You can get advice about your rights from a local Centre for Independent Living or from a local or national disability organisation. If you want to complain about any social care service providers, you should notify the relevant inspection agency.

You can talk to your local Citizens Advice bureau for help on how to make a complaint when things go wrong.
- ⓦ www.adviceguide.org.uk/england/ healthcare_e/healthcare_nhs_and_ adult_social_care_complaints.htm

For helpful tips on how to make a complaint from letter-writing and documenting the issue to what you can expect in response:
- ⓦ www.mind.org.uk/information- support/legal-rights/complaining- about-health-and-social-care

There are a variety of other ways of influencing health and social care services. Your local disabled people's organisation or centre for independent living will have suggestions.

The Motability Scheme enables disabled people to use their government-funded mobility allowance to lease a new car, scooter or powered wheelchair.

Today, over 630,000 disabled people and their families benefit from the freedom and independence provided through the Motability Scheme. People like five-year-old Joshua and his parents. Joshua loves playing with his toy dinosaurs and enjoys going to the zoo and museums to learn more about animals. Joshua has Caudal Regression Syndrome and Sacral Agenesis, resulting in him not being able to move or use his legs.

"Before we found out about Motability, we were using a family member's minibus to travel in, which was extremely expensive to run and became unsuitable," says Joshua's mum Victoria. We found out about the Motability Scheme and realised that we could use Joshua's mobility allowance to pay for a reliable car including insurance, breakdown cover and servicing.

"Joshua uses a wheelchair now and it is so important to have a vehicle that is reliable and can fit all of his equipment in safely. We have so much more freedom now as a family and we appreciate all the help that we have received from Motability."

If you receive any of the following benefits, and have at least 12 months' award length remaining when you apply, you may be able to join the Motability Scheme:

- Higher Rate Mobility Component of the Disability Living Allowance
- Enhanced Rate Mobility Component of the Personal Independence Payment
- Armed Forces Independence Payment
- War Pensioners' Mobility Supplement.

You simply exchange all or part of your allowance to lease a car, Wheelchair Accessible Vehicle (WAV),scooter or powered wheelchair of your choice. Vehicle adaptations are also available, many at no extra cost, to make your travelling experience safer or more comfortable. Motability is a national charity which oversees the Motability Scheme and may be able to provide financial help if you are unable to afford the car, adaptations or WAV you need.

All cars, scooters and powered wheelchairs provided under the Motability Scheme are leased to customers by Motability Operations Limited which is authorised and regulated by the Financial Conduct Authority.

For more information, call 0300 456 4566 or visit motability.co.uk

Getting around

Travel by people with disabilities and health conditions is on the rise. The travel industry is waking up to disabled travellers' needs by providing more inclusive and accessible services. Meanwhile, information about accessible travel is easier to find – much of it generated by disabled travellers themselves. This can help to build confidence. Getting out and about can increase our opportunities to do the things we want.

Travel and mobility

Getting around is crucial for all of us: getting to school, college or work; going to meet friends; to the cinema or to do sport or a hobby. Unfortunately, the degree of inclusion available in London doesn't exist everywhere, and access problems on older trains and rural buses are still common for those with mobility impairments.

And travelling, whether for a short distance commute or for a longer journey, can create anxiety for all of us. If you have mobility difficulties, sensory impairments, a learning disability, or a mental or other health condition, public transport hasn't always been that user-friendly.

However, transport and travel systems are gradually changing to become more accessible to everyone. There is still a way to go, and being well-informed is important. But often it can be done – and there is a range of information and support services to help.

There are also benefits and schemes designed to help disabled people overcome the barriers to getting out and about.

In more and more places people with disabilities and health conditions are successfully becoming involved in the training of bus drivers and some rail company staff.

When I left school in 1965, there was not an accessible taxi in the country. If I travelled by rail I was placed into a dark, cold and dreary guard's van. The only accessible vehicles were owned by charities. None of the pavements were ramped so it was impossible to get to the bus stop – but then none of the buses were accessible.

During the last two decades much of public transport in the UK has become accessible to disabled people.

Sir Bert Massie CBE

There are innovative ideas such as the First Group and Blackpool Transport model 'Safe Journey' card, which allows people to personalise and show to bus drivers and rail staff their particular access needs – from asking the driver to face you because of your hearing impairment, to giving you a bit longer to sit down before moving away. This project is being led by the Disability Action Alliance, along with other major bus operators. Through it people are being empowered to make their journeys safer and more enjoyable.

For information about how to get financial support for mobility through social security benefits, see the money chapter.

Feeling confident

A lack of confidence is one of the most difficult things about travel when you have a disability or health condition. There are so many stories about things going wrong and lots of people cite transport as one of the biggest barriers that they face.

A traveller's tale

"If I've not done a journey before, I ask someone to come with me the first time if possible. This helps me concentrate on remembering my way and the different elements of the journey. I try to travel outside of rush hour wherever possible. I still have to steel myself to do it. I've had panic attacks on buses and on the underground. But I tell myself that it will be worth it – I want to lead my life."

Of course, our experiences will vary hugely, depending upon our circumstances – including where we live: urban or rural; market town or tiny village.

Many transport companies have made significant progress in recent years. For example, as a wheelchair user spontaneous travel is now more possible. It used to be the case that you had to give 48 hours notice. Some travel systems, such as the Docklands Light Railway, have schemes where you can 'try a journey' with a mentor.

Getting the planning right

Being well-informed is the basis of confident travel.

Transport Direct

A good place to start is the Transport Direct website which helps you to find various routes for a particular journey. You can compare them in terms of cost, time and effect on the environment.
Ⓦ www.transportdirect.info

Traveline

If you are planning to use public transport, check out the Traveline website which was created by a partnership of transport operators and local authorities to provide impartial and comprehensive information. It links you to journey planners for regional public transport networks all over the country so you can find out what's available in your area. They also provide telephone support (10p per minute plus any charges your network provider makes).
Ⓣ 0871 200 22 33
Ⓦ http://traveline.info

In major urban areas, look at the websites of the local Passenger Transport Executive (PTE):

Transport for London
Ⓦ www.tfl.gov.uk
Transport for Greater Manchester
Ⓦ www.tfgm.gov.uk
West Midlands – Centro
Ⓦ www.centro.org.uk
Merseyside – MerseyTravel
Ⓦ www.merseytravel.gov.uk
West Yorkshire – Metro
Ⓦ www.wymetro.com
South Yorkshire – South Yorkshire PTE
Ⓦ www.sypte.co.uk
Tyne & Wear – Nexus
Ⓦ www.nexus.org.uk
Greater Glasgow – Strathclyde Passenger Transport
Ⓦ www.spt.co.uk
Northern Ireland
Ⓦ www.translink.co.uk

Many will have their own journey planners such as this one from Transport for London. The Advanced Search feature enables you to search by type of access needed.
Ⓦ http://journeyplanner.tfl.gov.uk

A traveller's tale
"I always use the journey planner. It's like putting on my shoes. Just part of going out. My arthritis makes it difficult. I'm quite young and I don't "look disabled" so I rarely get offered a seat. I like to know where there are seats on the platform, how many steps I'll have to deal with, the exactly distance if I go by different routes, that sort of thing."

Transport for London also has 'how to' films which show what it's like travelling in London and the facilities and assistance available. It can also arrange for a 'travel mentor' to come with you on a journey so you can test it out:
Ⓦ www.tfl.gov.uk/transport-accessibility

Direct Enquiries provides access information on all kinds of buildings, including those concerned with transport:
Ⓦ www.directenquiries.com

For the latest on travel, check BBC Travel News – the page is updated every few minutes and brings all road and public transport updates together.
Ⓦ www.bbc.co.uk/travelnews

It can also sometimes be useful to have information with you too. Not just for the time when you can't get internet access or a mobile phone signal but for when flicking through the timetable is just the easiest thing to do.

Most transport operators provide leaflets and hard copies of timetables as well as audio material such as DVDs and podcasts. If you can't pick these up from the transport provider's information centre or download them from the internet, ask for them to be posted to you. Maps are always useful.

Assume most people are helpful. It's a fact – good experiences far outweigh bad. Be clear what sort of help you want and, if you need a seat, making your disability visible to other passengers often helps.

MOBILES, SMARTPHONES AND APPS

Many transport operators will have mobile versions of their websites or apps. Check on their websites and at the appropriate app store for your phone.

Taking charge

Planning checklist

- Make sure you know how the transport systems you'll be using work.
- If you haven't bought tickets in advance, how do you buy tickets on the day?
- Can you get a reduction as, for example, a disabled or older traveller?
- During what time periods is your ticket valid?
- How can you ensure you'll get on the right train?
- Are you guaranteed a seat?
- How do you make sure you get a seat if you need one?
- Where will you find staff and what can you reasonably expect of them?
- How is information given?
- How will you find out about any delays or other problems?
- How will you find a route that's accessible to get you to the platform or stop?
- How do you book passenger assistance if needed?
- Are there accessible loos along the way?
- Will you be able to get anything to eat or drink if you need it?
- Can your personal assistant travel with you?

Transport Direct and Traveline are both available on your mobile or smartphone. NextBuses is a mobile internet service, also available as an iPhone or Android smartphone app, which will tell you the time of your next bus. Traveline-txt is a similar service whereby you can check the next buses by texting the code of a particular bus stop. The code and the number should appear somewhere on the bus stop, in the signage or timetable notice.

There's more information on both NextBuses and Traveline-txt on the Traveline site. For more information:

- Ⓦ http://traveline.info
- Ⓦ www.reading-buses.co.uk/mobile-bus-times

Direct Enquiries has a smartphone app, called 'Inclusive Britain':

- Ⓦ www.directenquiries.com

In London, you can check live bus times on computer, smartphone or by text by using bus stop codes. You'll find more on the Transport for London website.

- Ⓦ www.tfl.gov.uk

There are also apps and internet tools that can help you plan your journey and guide 'books' for when you get there. Many apps are free.

Technology is improving access to information all the time. For example, QRs (or mobile barcodes) are beginning to appear on bus stops to give travellers fuller access to timetables and information.

Travel by train

Give National Rail train companies advance notice, preferably 48 hours, if you think you'll need substantial help from staff.

ⓦ www.nationalrail.co.uk/passenger_services/disabled_passengers

To check if a station has accessible facilities.

ⓦ www.nationalrail.co.uk/stations

DISABLED PERSONS RAILCARD

If you're eligible you can get up to a third off the cost of rail tickets if you buy a Disabled Persons Railcard. You can apply online or by post and will need to provide photocopied or scanned evidence that you have one of the qualifying health conditions or disablities.

Disabled Persons Railcard Office
PO Box 6613 Arbroath DD11 9AN
ⓣ 0345 605 0525;
textphone 0345 601 0132
ⓦ www.disabledpersons-railcard.co.uk

What do you get and what does it cost?
You get one-third off most rail fares throughout Great Britain for you and an adult companion. It currently costs £20 for a one-year or £54 for a three-year Railcard.

Are you eligible?
You may qualify if you:
- receive a disability-related benefit, including Personal Independence Payment
- are registered as deaf or use a hearing aid
- are registered as visually impaired
- have epilepsy.

I have had my Railcard for six years ... Living on disability benefits is not easy but I save so much on train travel, I have the funds to go to the theatre, galleries, exhibitions, a little more often.

Genevieve Barr says: "I live and work in London and with my acting, work in disability and leadership, I travel a lot. I like overground trains best – they're spacious and very accessible with live information written on screens as well as voiced over.

Of course, trains can frustrate me. Information about delays is only relayed by microphone and that means that because I am deaf I have to ask someone ... or suffer in silence. I also like the tube because it is fast and the information is really clear and easy to use. I do think it can be made much more accessible though, particularly for wheelchair users."

Travel by car

A car can bring you great independence if you have limited mobility or public transport remains inaccessible to you because of fatigue, pain or anxiety.

BLUE BADGE SCHEME

The Blue Badge scheme helps disabled drivers and passengers to park closer to their destinations.

You can use this online portal to make an application.
- Ⓦ www.gov.uk/apply-blue-badge

Blue Badge Initial Enquiry Support Service:
- Ⓦ bluebadge@northgate-is.com
- Ⓣ 0844 463 0213 (England)
  0844 463 0214 (Scotland)
  0844 463 0215 (Wales)

Find out more information about the Blue Badge scheme from your local council.
- Ⓦ www.gov.uk/blue-badge-scheme-information-council

MOTABILITY SCHEME

The Motability Scheme gives disabled people the chance to lease a car, scooter or powered wheelchair at an affordable price, using one of the following benefits:
- the higher rate mobility component of Disability Living Allowance
- the enhanced rate mobility component of Personal Independence Payment
- War Pensioners' Mobility Supplement
- Armed Forces Independence Payment.

Contact Motability to find out more:
- Ⓣ 0845 456 4566;
  textphone 0845 675 0009
- Ⓦ www.motability.co.uk

ADAPTING YOUR VEHICLE

You get an independent assessment of your adaptation needs through the Forum of Mobility Centres.

Find out more about adapting your vehicle and where to get special controls fitted through from Ricability.
- Ⓦ www.ricability.org.uk/consumer_reports/mobility_reports/car_controls

VEHICLE EXCISE DUTY EXEMPTION

You are exempt from Vehicle Excise Duty (road tax) if you are receiving one of the following benefits:
- the higher rate mobility component of Disability Living Allowance (DLA)
- the enhanced rate mobility component of Personal Independence Payment (PIP)
- War Pensioners' Mobility Supplement
- Armed Forces Independence Payment (AFIP).

If you receive the standard rate mobility component of PIP, you will be entitled to a 50% discount.

When you are awarded the appropriate rate of DLA or PIP, you should also receive a re-useable 'Certificate of Entitlement' for Vehicle Excise Duty exemption.

If you receive the War Pensioner's Mobility Supplement or the AFIP, you will need to apply for one – contact the Service Personnel and Veterans Agency:
- ☎ 0800 169 2277;
  textphone 0800 169 3458

HEALTH CONDITIONS, DISABILITIES AND DRIVING

For many people with health conditions and disabilities, the ability to drive is liberating. We can be in charge of our mobility and go far further than we might be able to travel on foot or by wheelchair or scooter. It may also be essential for our job or parenting or caring responsibilities.

A driver's tale

"My usual GP was away on maternity leave when my driving licence came up for renewal at 70. The locum felt that I shouldn't be driving because of my heart pills and told that to the DVLA. I was devastated. I live in quite a rural area but I wasn't ready to give up the car and move – I've got lovely neighbours. Luckily, my usual GP was soon back from leave. She gave a second opinion and between us we sorted it all out. I'm glad I didn't just give in!"

Fitness to drive

For safety reasons, you may need to tell DVLA if you have particular health conditions or medical treatments and you have a driving licence.

If your doctor thinks that you shouldn't drive for a health-related reason, whether because of epilepsy, or having had a mental health crisis or because of a physical impairment, you can ask for a second opinion about your fitness to drive.

You may be able to show that you are managing your condition and that it is now safe to drive. If possible, it is best to try to get a second opinion as soon as you can. The DVLA is likely to give your doctor's opinion a lot of weight and so it is better to get a second opinion before the DVLA comes to a decision.

If you disagree with a decision made by the DVLA regarding your licence, you can appeal to your local magistrates' court within six months of the decision.

To read the current DVLA medical standards for 'fitness to drive':
- 🌐 www.gov.uk/current-medical-guidelines-dvla-guidance-for-professionals

The independence that I gain from being able to travel allows me to do the things necessary for my recovery such as attending treatment appointments, socialising and volunteering.

If you have further evidence about your fitness to drive, you should bring it to the attention of the DVLA as soon as you can. You may be able to resolve the issue without going to court.

If you do decide to appeal, the first step is to contact your local magistrates' court for further information on the procedure. You need to inform the DVLA that you are appealing and you may wish to seek independent legal advice. You can find your nearest court by searching online at:

- W https://courttribunalfinder.service.gov.uk/search

You can use the email service to contact DVLA about driving and medical issues:

- W https://emaildvla.direct.gov.uk/emaildvla/cegemail/dvla/en/index.html

Drivers Medical Enquiries

Drivers Medical Enquiries, DVLA, Swansea SA99 1TU

T 0300 790 6806
Lines open Monday to Friday, 8am to 5:30pm and Saturday, 8am to 1pm

F 0845 850 0095

TOLL CONCESSIONS

You may be able to pay a reduced rate or nothing at some river crossings, bridges and tunnels if you're disabled. In most cases, you have to apply in advance to get a concession.

Toll concessions can change – check before you travel.

For more information:

- W www.mobility-centres.org.uk
- W www.focusondisability.org.uk

Some of the bridges and tunnels for which concessions are available:

- Cleddau Bridge (A477 Pembroke Dock)
- Clifton Suspension Bridge (B3129 Bristol)
- Dartford – Thurrock River Crossing (River Thames – A282/M25 Junction 1a)
- Humber Bridge (near Hull)
- Itchen Bridge (A3025 Woolston-Southampton)
- M6 Motorway (Birmingham Toll)
- Mersey Tunnel (Liverpool-Wirral)
- Severn Bridge (M48 England – Wales)
- Second Severn Crossing (M4 England – Wales)
- Tamar Bridge (A38 Plymouth-Liskeard)
- Torpoint Ferry (A374 Plymouth-Torpoint)
- Tyne Tunnel (near Newcastle)
- Whitchurch Bridge (B471 Pangbourne-Whitchurch).

Travel by bus or coach

On buses, there is usually at least one space for a wheelchair or scooter, but it's often shared with buggies and luggage. The wheelchair or scooter user should take priority – but it can be difficult to make that happen, especially if people are pretending not to notice you.

Often there is a notice and you can politely point it out and say something like: "Would you mind folding up your buggy so I can travel safely? Thanks." Try to say it quite loudly – people may be more willing to do what you ask if others are watching. You could ask the driver to help too.

> If you need a designated space that is being occupied by a buggy or other passengers, ask for it.

USING A WHEELCHAIR OR SCOOTER ON THE BUS

By 2017 most buses will be able to accommodate wheelchair users and by 2020 most coaches will. Coaches will require a forward-facing wheelchair space fitted with a wheelchair restraint system and wheelchair user restraint. Buses can continue to use rearward-facing, unrestrained positions.

The regulations setting out what 'accessible' means in practice are based on the design of the more usual types of wheelchair (and bus axle) so you may have problems if your wheelchair is heavy or takes up a lot of space. This may affect you if, for example, you need to travel with your legs fully extended or the backrest reclined. If you can, check it out with the bus operator.

A campaigner's tale
Gwynneth Pedler, Disability, transport and highways campaigner says: "Have you noticed the new markings on the floor of the Oxford Bus Company buses? We must congratulate them on addressing the problem of wheelchair users being frequently denied the use of the wheelchair space due to pushchairs, luggage and shopping. The markings quite clearly identify one side of the bus for pushchairs and the other for wheelchairs."

You're responsible for the travelworthiness of your wheelchair, for ensuring that its battery is secure and that its parts do not damage the ramp.

A transport operator has the right to refuse to take your wheelchair if they believe it is not safe for you or other passengers. It makes sense to check with the operator beforehand if there is any doubt about the suitability of your wheelchair. Once on the bus, you must make sure your wheelchair brakes are on and that the power on a powered wheelchair is switched off.

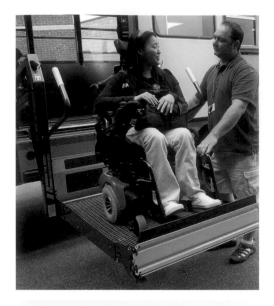

"The advances in making transport more accessible for disabled people have changed my life dramatically. It has given me and my family a way to travel and the opportunity to get out.

Before buses were made accessible with the wheelchair space, I had been confined to a large adult buggy and was forced to always travel with a companion. I now have the freedom to travel short distances (that are well tried and tested) independently and am able to meet people at the other end without them being obliged to travel with me.

This has greatly improved my confidence and my view of the outside and my place in it. It most certainly contributed to my choice and ability to travel in to London to both study and now to work. Without these advances this would have been extremely difficult."

HELP GETTING ON AND OFF

The law says bus and coach drivers must give reasonable assistance to disabled people, such as helping us get on and off the bus or coach. This doesn't mean physically lifting passengers or heavy mobility equipment.

If you need help to get on and off a coach, you should ask for this when you book your ticket.

BUS PASSES

In most areas of the UK, you can get a bus pass for free travel if you qualify on grounds of age, health or disability. In some areas, these passes are also valid for train, tram or underground travel (time restrictions may apply).

Some authorities allow qualifying holders of a disabled pass to be accompanied by a companion who is entitled to free travel when accompanying the pass holder.

Applying for a bus pass
Contact your local council to find out the specific age and disability-related conditions and make an application:

In England and Wales:
Ⓦ www.gov.uk/apply-for-disabled-bus-pass

In Scotland:
Ⓦ www.transportscotland.gov.uk

In Northern Ireland:
Ⓦ www.nidirect.gov.uk/free-bus-travel-and-concessions

Travel by taxi or minicab

Licensed taxis can be hailed on the street, picked up at ranks or pre-booked, but you can only pre-book minicabs (also called 'private hire vehicles').

WHEELCHAIR ACCESS

In some areas (mainly larger cities), licensed taxis have to be wheelchair accessible. To find out if there are accessible taxis near you, contact the taxi licensing office at your local council.
ⓦ www.gov.uk/find-your-local-council

Some of the newer 'black cabs' are also fitted with induction loops and intercoms for hearing aid users.

ASSISTANCE DOGS

If you travel with an assistance dog they must be allowed into the taxi or minicab with you, unless the driver has an exemption certificate. This can be issued if they've got a medical condition made worse by contact with dogs.

A driver with an exemption certificate will have a yellow 'Notice of Exemption' notice on their vehicle windscreen.

It's illegal to be charged extra to travel in a taxi or minicab with an assistance dog. Otherwise the driver could be fined up to £1000.

The following types of dog can be taken with you in taxis or minicabs:
- guide dogs trained by the Guide Dogs organisation
- hearing dogs trained by Hearing Dogs
- assistance dogs trained by Dogs for the Disabled, Support Dogs or Canine Partners.

Travelling with your dog
Taxi and private hire vehicle drivers have been told how to identify assistance dogs. Your assistance dog should wear its harness or identification jacket when you are travelling with it. If an identification card was issued for the dog, this should also be carried.

Dogs should remain on the floor and under control at all times. If your dog causes any damage to the vehicle, the driver could ask you to pay for it.

REPORTING PROBLEMS

As well as the rules on wheelchairs and assistance dogs, all taxi and minicab drivers must make sure they don't discriminate against you and can't treat you less favourably than other customers.

They should also make any 'reasonable adjustments' to their service for you to make your journey easier.

You should report any problems to the taxi licensing office at your local council.
ⓦ www.gov.uk/find-your-local-council

Travel by tram

There are a number of tramway/ light rail systems in Britain, such as in Birmingham, Blackpool, Croydon, London's docklands, Manchester, Newcastle, Nottingham and Sheffield.
Ⓦ www.thetrams.co.uk/tramsinuk.php

Your local Passenger Transport Executive will include details of whether trams are available, their accessibility and the routes they cover.

Travel by tube/underground/ metro

Birmingham, Blackpool, Edinburgh, Llandudno, London, Greater Manchester, Newcastle, Nottingham, Southport and Sheffield all have metro systems.

London's underground travel system ('the tube') was mostly built over 100 years ago and access is difficult to many parts of the network. However, there are a number of newer lines that have reasonable or good access. A 'step-free' map and information about facilities and assistance can be found in the 'Transport accessibility' section of the Transport for London website.
Ⓦ www.tfl.gov.uk

Transport for All is an organisation of disabled and older people. It ensures that the experiences and opinions of travellers in London are heard by those who commission and run the transport network.
Ⓦ www.transportforall.org.uk

Glasgow also has a 'subway' system:
Ⓦ www.spt.co.uk/subway

The tube can be crowded and in the summer extremely hot. If you can, travel outside peak times and, if you need to, ask for a seat. It's helpful to have water with you in the summer.

A traveller's tale
"I like the tube because it is fast and the information is really clear and easy to use. I do think it can be made much more accessible though, particularly for wheelchair users. Still, public transport is getting there."

Travel by air

Tell your airline about your disability at least 48 hours before departure if you'll need help. Airlines and airports have different facilities for disabled people.

Find out from your airport or airline if they have the facilities you need, such as a toilet with disabled access.

HELP AT THE AIRPORT

If you have a sensory, physical or learning disability which affects your mobility when using transport, at European airports you have the right to:
- help at specific arrival points, such as at terminal entrances, at transport interchanges and in car parks
- help to reach check-in
- help with registration at check-in
- help with moving through the airport, including to toilets if you need it.

You'll also have the right to help because of your age or a temporary illness or injury – for example because you've broken your leg and it's in a cast.

As a disabled person, you can travel with two items of mobility equipment free of charge. This won't count as part of your baggage allowance.

FLYING WITH YOUR WHEELCHAIR

You can't take your own wheelchair into the passenger cabin of a plane – it will be stored in the hold. Speak to your airline to find out what help they'll provide when boarding.

You should tell your airline, travel agent or tour operator as soon as possible if you're taking on a battery-powered wheelchair or mobility aid.

TRAVELLING WITH A COMPANION

You may need to travel with someone in some circumstances, for example if, you need help with eating, breathing, using medication or using the loo.

The airline you're flying with will do their best to make sure you sit next to each other, so long as you tell them at least 48 hours before departure.

> The Equality and Human Rights Commission publishes *Your rights to fly: a step by step guide*. You can download it from the 'Your rights' section of their website.
> Ⓦ www.equalityhumanrights.com

TRAVELLING WITH AN ASSISTANCE DOG

You have the right to travel with your assistance dog. You'll need to follow the rules on pet travel.
Ⓦ www.gov.uk/take-pet-abroad/overview

Useful publications
- Disability Rights UK's *Doing Transport Differently* – a guide about public transport for everyone with a disability or health conditions.
- Disability Rights UK's *Holidays in the British Isles – a guide for disabled people*
- *Time Out Open London*: a guide to accessible London.

Travel by ferry

A ferry, whether as a foot passenger or taking your car, can be a good way to travel abroad.

A good website for comparing companies and prices is:
Ⓦ www.spt.co.uk/subway

Direct ferries' website enables you to find out what it's like on board before you travel, with ship guides, on board videos and ferry reviews, which can help remove the anxiety of travelling.
Ⓦ www.directferries.co.uk

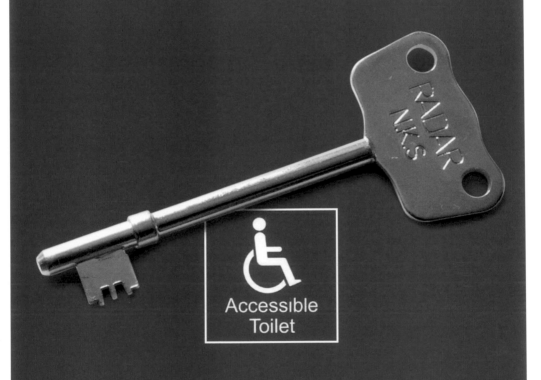

Would you like priority access to over 9000 accessible UK toilets?

Accessible Toilet

The answer is a Radar key

With your own Radar key you can unlock most disabled toilets in the UK

Accessible toilets

An accessible toilet is a toilet designed to accommodate people who have disabilities and health conditions.

Public toilets and restrooms can present accessibility difficulties for people with disabilities, especially those in wheelchairs. Stalls may not be able to fit a wheelchair, and transferring between the wheelchair and the toilet seat may pose a challenge.

Your rights

In the United Kingdom, the Equality Act requires individuals and organisations providing services to the public to make adjustments to meet the needs of disabled people.

Accessible toilets are designed to address these issues by providing more space and bars for users to grab and hold during transfers.

THE RADAR KEY

The Radar key opens more than 9000 accessible toilets in the UK. The first Radar toilet opened in 1981. Since then, more than 400 local authorities and thousands of businesses have joined this national key scheme.

The National Key Scheme

Radar keys are for people who need the use of accessible toilet facilities because of their disability or health condition. For more information or to buy your own key, visit the Disability Rights UK online shop:

Ⓦ www.disabilityrightsuk.org

The scheme was first created so that disabled people could have access to toilets, specifically for their own use, in public areas, office blocks, pubs or restaurants. Having a locked toilet ensures it is not misused by other users. Owning a key prevents the delay or embarrassment of needing to ask for one.

CHANGING PLACES TOILETS

Standard accessible toilets do not meet the needs of all people with a health condition or disability.

People with profound and multiple learning disabilities, as well as other impairments such as spinal injuries, muscular dystrophy, multiple sclerosis or an acquired brain injury, often need extra facilities to allow them to use toilets comfortably.

Changing Places toilets are different to standard accessible toilets with extra features and more space to meet these needs. There are currently over 500 around the UK and the Changing Places Consortium is campaigning for more to be installed in key public buildings.

Each Changing Places toilet provides:

- the right equipment (a height adjustable adult-sized changing bench and a tracking hoist system or mobile hoist)
- adequate space in the changing area for the disabled person and up to two carers
- a centrally placed toilet with room either side for the carers
- a screen or curtain to provide some privacy

- a safe and clean environment (a washbasin, wide tear off paper roll to cover the bench, a large waste bin for disposable pads, and a non-slip floor).

Changing Places toilets
To find the location, access details and opening times of Changing Places toilets visit the *Find a toilet* section of their website:
Ⓦ www.changing-places.org

A campaigner's tale

Samantha Buck is a mum of three whose youngest son is seven years old and was born with quadriplegic cerebral palsy (massive brain damage) due to being starved of oxygen at birth.

"We go into town on a regular basis to shop, have lunch, and meet up with other mums for coffee with their disabled children/teenagers in the same situation. When he was five years old we were given a Radar key to access the disabled toilets in Horsham which I was very pleased with, until I actually used the disabled toilet.

I realised that 'disabled loos' are not for the severely disabled or elderly, they are for the limping, walking with sticks or wheelchair users with upper mobility, who can get themselves onto a toilet. If you are severely disabled or paralysed, you need carers to lift you out of the wheelchair and place you on a flat surface to have your continence pad changed.

This is what I do with my seven year old son. I have often had to lay him on a urine soaked floor inside the disabled loo, with the second carer standing outside with the wheelchair. They have to pass me the changing accessories through the open door for all passersby to view.

This is one of the most awful experiences I have to face every time I come into Horsham Town.

I approached our local council, MP and councillors, and posted a picture of my son lying on the toilet floor on our Town Facebook Page and, 'boom', people had no idea that severely disabled people have this awful situation to deal with.

Then people wanted to do a story. I have been on BBC Sussex and Surrey Radio, Spirit Fm, and BBC South Today News on the TV, since then our home town are putting in two Changing Places toilets – but it is mostly up to the families to approach their local Council and rally awareness."

Wheelchairs

See the equipment chapter and the section on Motability earlier in this chapter for information about wheelchairs.

Taking charge

Getting out!

A 'dropped kerb' outside your home may make it easier to get from your car to your house or to get out and about easily in your wheelchair. It involves lowering the kerbstones and making a small ramp from the road to your pavement or driveway. To apply for a dropped kerb:

If you live in England and Wales:
Ⓦ www.gov.uk/apply-dropped-kerb

In Northern Ireland:
Ⓦ www.nidirect.gov.uk/applying-for-a-dropped-kerb

In Scotland:
Ⓦ www.directscot.org/article/applying-for-a-dropped-kerb#

Community transport services and Shopmobility

Many areas have community transport services for people who have difficulty using public transport. These include door-to-door transport and trips to shopping centres.

Shopmobility lends wheelchairs and powered scooters to people who are disabled so they can shop or visit leisure facilities in a town, city or shopping centre.

In England and Wales, you can use this online portal to find out about eligibility and contacts.
Ⓦ www.gov.uk/community-transport-services-shopmobility

Useful resources

Visit Britain has useful information about getting around Britain in the *Transport* section of their website:
Ⓦ www.visitbritain.com/en/Transport/Getting-around-Britain/Getting-around-Britain-with-access-or-disabled-needs.htm

Travelling abroad

This guide relates principally to Britain but travelling abroad involves many of the same principles of planning and building your confidence by being well-informed.

When contacting holiday providers, airlines, hotels etc, if appropriate, clearly state your needs and what help you want. Just telling people you have a particular disability doesn't mean that they will understand your needs, so clearly explain them.

The Association of British Travel Agents provides a *Checklist for Disabled and Less Mobile Passengers* which can be downloaded from their website:
Ⓦ www.abta.com/consumer-services/accessible_travel

Confirm enquiries, bookings and reservations in writing and double check all arrangements before departure.

The Foreign Office provides general information about travelling to different countries:

Ⓦ www.gov.uk/knowbeforeyougo

It also produces a guide specifically for disabled travellers:

Ⓦ www.gov.uk/government/uploads/ system/uploads/attachment_data/ file/265603/DisabledTravellers_1113_ AW.pdf

Your rights
UN CONVENTION ON THE RIGHTS OF PERSONS WITH DISABILITIES
Article 20 of the United Nations Convention on the Rights of Persons with Disabilities says:

Government should do everything possible to ensure disabled people can get around as independently as possible, including by:
* ensuring people can travel when they want at a price they can afford
* ensuring people have access to quality, affordable mobility aids including new technology or help from other people to help them get around
* providing mobility training to disabled people and staff working with them
* encouraging manufacturers of mobility aids and technologies to think about all aspects of mobility for disabled persons.

This means that the government and public bodies should take steps so that disabled people can get around, in the way they want to – disabled people should be able to decide for themselves what this might be.

When planning for a transport infrastructure, public authorities should think about how disabled people are affected, particularly those who rely on one type of transport.

You could use this Article to highlight the need for public bodies to think about affordable mobility aids. For example, blind people often have to pay for a white stick. Providers of mobility aids should also think about the purpose of the mobility aids. For example, a wheelchair centre should include in their assessment where the wheelchair user wants to go – and what they like to do (for example, do they do sports; do they travel abroad).

Taking charge

Using the UN Convention
A local council provides transport for people with learning disabilities between their home and a day centre.

If one person or a group wants to visit a museum, then they still have to come to the day centre first, where transport will be provided to the museum, and back to the centre. However this means that there is not much time for the actual visit to the museum.

The users of the day centre could use Article 20 (with Article 30 which is the right to take part in culture) to say that the council should enable them to travel directly from their home to the museum – for example by giving travel training.

THE PUBLIC SERVICE VEHICLE ACCESSIBILITY REGULATIONS 2000

These regulations apply to all new public service vehicles (buses or coaches) introduced since 31 December 2000 with a capacity exceeding 22 passengers used to provide a local or scheduled service. They apply in England, Scotland and Wales. Northern Ireland has introduced separate regulations.

According to these regulations:
- All full size single deck buses over 7.5 tonnes will be fully accessible from 1 January 2016, and all double deck buses from 1 January 2017.
- New buses weighing up to 7.5 tonnes and coaches have been wheelchair accessible since 2005.
- All buses weighing up to 7.5 tonnes are fully accessible from 1 January 2015 and coaches by 1 January 2020.

THE RAIL VEHICLE ACCESSIBILITY REGULATIONS (RVAR)

These regulations apply to all new rail vehicles entering service in Great Britain since 31 December 1998.

This includes, for example, providing access for wheelchair users, the size and location of handrails, handholds and control devices as well as providing passenger information systems and other equipment.

All rail vehicles, both heavy and light rail, must be accessible by no later than 1 January 2020.

EQUALITY ACT 2010

The Equality Act 2010 protects disabled people from disability discrimination in access to goods and services including land-based transport services. This includes access to railway and bus stations. The Equality Act applies to people with invisible impairments as well as visible ones.

Transport companies are obliged by law to make 'reasonable adjustments' to eliminate problems such as poorly presented timetables, over-complex booking procedures, inadequate or inaccessible facilities, lack of assistance for disabled people etc.

Your right to reasonable adjustments could include providing timetables, fare tariffs or other information in an accessible format. Most operators do this and more.

The government is advised on disability and transport issues by the Disabled Persons Transport Advisory Committee, an independent body set up by the Transport Act 1985.

The public sector equality duty in the Equality Act requires public bodies including transport providers to have due regard to eliminating discrimination and promoting equality of opportunity when developing or implementing policy.

You also have rights under the European Passenger Rights Regulations affecting air, rail, ferry, bus and coach travel. These apply across Europe not just in the UK. For more information visit:
- ⓦ http://ec.europa.eu/passengerrights

A campaigner's tale

Doug Paulley from Wetherby, West Yorkshire took First Bus Group to court after he was told he could not get on a bus because a pushchair user refused to give up the space.

A judge at Leeds County Court ruled the 'first come first served' policy was unlawful discrimination in breach of the Equality Act 2010.

Mr Paulley said "Somebody with a pushchair in the wheelchair space refused to move when asked by the driver, because their baby was asleep in the pushchair and they didn't want to wake the baby up. So I was unable to get on the bus, I was told to get off the bus and wait for the next one."

In December 2014 the Court of Appeal overturned this judgment – though they did emphasise the need for drivers to take reasonable steps to ensure disabled people could use the space, like asking others to move and potentially not driving off until they did. In 2015 this important case was heading for the Supreme Court

DISABLED PEOPLE'S PROTECTION POLICIES

Your right to travel by train is protected by the train company's Disabled People's Protection Policy (DPPP). Each train company must produce a DPPP and you can get a copy from the company.

The DPPP explains how the train company helps disabled passengers use their stations and trains.

Complaints

When anyone is travelling, there's always a risk that they will encounter problems – delayed or cancelled trains or buses, accessible toilets that are out of use and airlines that leave passengers stranded on the runway.

When the worst happens, it's important to know where you can turn to make a complaint, particularly if the company concerned has failed to resolve a situation to your satisfaction.

In some areas, there are specific bodies set up to deal with complaints. For example, London TravelWatch is the voice of London's transport users and the statutory appeals body. If you have a complaint or problem with any aspect of transport in London and the surrounding area, they can help.

They examine all complaints bought to them by people who are unhappy with responses they have received from their transport or service provider, and seek redress on their behalf.
- Ⓦ www.londontravelwatch.org.uk/complaints

In some cases, where the transport complaint relates to the local council, for example in relation to school transport, you can take a complaint to the Local Government Ombudsman:
- Ⓦ www.lgo.org.uk

If all else fails, take your complaint to small claims court. For more information about how to take legal action visit the *Consumer* section of Adviceguide:
- Ⓦ www.adviceguide.org.uk

Learning and working

Education and employment enable us to develop our talents, earn a living, meet new people, achieve goals and contribute to society. People with health conditions and disabilities often have fantastic skills and insights to share in learning and work environments. Qualifications can make a big difference to your employment prospects and learning can also be its own reward. Employers increasingly recognise our talents.

This chapter tells you what you have a right to expect in education, employment and making a contribution as a volunteer or community or public leader.

Education

Pupils, students and those who want to learn have the right not to be discriminated against because of disability or health. They also have the right to 'reasonable adjustments' to help make learning possible. These rights are for people who have a health condition or disability in childhood and those who acquire them in later life.

The rights cover:
- admissions
- the curriculum, teaching and learning and other services provided wholly or mainly for pupils and students – including school trips and outings, school sports, leisure facilities and school meals, libraries and learning centres, work experience and student accommodation
- exclusion from an education institution or course.

Reasonable adjustments in post-16 education include providing auxiliary aids and services and removing or altering physical features of buildings that create barriers.

SCHOOL

Understanding how you can exercise your rights or what 'reasonable adjustment' at school means will depend on your circumstances.

There are a huge range of adaptations, adjustments and teaching aids that can support pupils with health conditions and/or disabilities.

I am perfectly capable of doing everything that the other school kids do. It just needs an adjustment to the situation to make me able to do it as well.

It is unlawful for a school to charge you for making a reasonable adjustment in any circumstances. For example, an independent school provides a pupil who has dyslexia and autism with coloured overlay sheets, which help him to read text, and weekly sessions with a specialist teacher. If the school added the cost of these adjustments to the pupil's school fees, this would be unlawful discrimination.

It was the most important moment of my life. For the first time I could see text clear as glass. I was astounded ... All I could think to say was 'How did they do that?'

ADDITIONAL NEEDS

All state pre-schools, nurseries, schools and local authorities must try to identify and help assess children with educational, health and social needs.

If you think your child might have special educational needs, contact the SEN co-ordinator or SENCO at your child's school.

If your child needs more support than is available through special educational needs support, you can ask your local authority to carry out an education, health and care (EHC) assessment.

The local authority will then decide whether to create an EHC plan for your child and what additional support will be made available to meet their educational, health and social care needs up to the age of 25.

This government website is a good place to find out how to get their needs assessed and some of the support available:

Ⓦ www.gov.uk/children-with-special-educational-needs

Supporting the whole child

The Children and Families Act 2014 is focused on integrating all relevant services so that children defined as having SEN are consistently supported towards the best outcomes for them.

The SEN system now extends from birth to the age of 25, giving children, young people and their parents greater control and choice in decisions and in ensuring needs are met. It replaces the old SEN statements with a new birth to 25 'education, health and care' plan.

It offers families personal budgets to meet needs. It involves cooperation between all the services that support children and their families, particularly requiring local authorities and health services to work together.

Information Advice and Support (IAS) Services provide free, impartial advice and support to parents and carers of children and young people with SEN. There should be an IAS Service in every local authority in England. To find the contact details of your local service:

- ☎ 020 7843 1900
- 🅦 www.iassnetwork.org.uk/find-your-iass

Challenging 'risk'
Schools should not make uninformed assumptions about you, your needs or the risks.

Arlo, a pupil with a stair-climbing wheelchair, applied to a large secondary school with several flights of stairs. The school wanted to stop him from using the stair-climbing wheelchair in the school as they thought it would be dangerous. His parents insisted on an independent risk assessment and the school realised that it did not present a significant risk and so it would be reasonable for them to allow him to use it.

Inclusive education
The Centre for Studies on Inclusive Education (CSIE) works to promote equality and eliminate discrimination in education. They do research, provide training, deliver workshops and produce a wide range of resources and publications to inform and support inclusive education for children, young people and adults.

- 🅦 www.csie.org.uk

Rights in practice
In 2013, 10-year-old Thomas Pettigrew, a disabled pupil from East Kilbride, won a tribunal that meant he could attend guitar classes at school. Thomas was keen to join the after-school guitar club; he could hold and play the guitar but needed additional help lifting and storing the instrument and turning the sheet music; he also needed help to go to the loo. Thomas's mother requested additional support after school so he could attend the guitar club but South Lanarkshire Council refused.

The tribunal found the council had failed to make reasonable adjustments; that Thomas was substantially disadvantaged in engaging in guitar club; and that his health and safety were compromised as a result, as he was left without support to go to the loo.

After the case, Thomas's mother said: "We can finally move forward and get it right for Thomas. It is important that Thomas can now learn to do something he loves, just like his friends, and also that other parents know that this type of support is available to them".

Into Apprenticeships
The guide for disabled people

Doing an apprenticeship is a great way to earn a salary, get qualifications and develop your career. This guide is designed to help disabled people, parents and advisers answer the key questions about applying for apprenticeships in England.

The guide includes:

- The benefits of an apprenticeship, how to apply, find vacancies, and what support is available in the workplace
- Case studies where disabled students write about their own experiences
- A resources section listing helpful websites, publications and organisations

Free to download

Printed copies £3.99

"The stories written by disabled apprentices about their experiences are really inspiring and we hope this guide will help you make the right choices and get the support you need."

Tony Stevens, Careers guidance specialist and adviser

You can buy our publications online at www.disabilityrightsuk.org

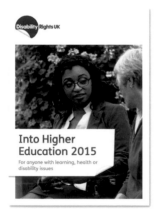

Into Higher Education 2015
For anyone with learning, health or disability issues

This guide is designed to help disabled students make the right decisions about studying in higher education. It deals with common questions: whether the college or university will be accessible, how to choose a course and what support will be available.

The guide includes:

- The student finance system, tuition fees, repayment methods and the support that will be in place
- Case studies where disabled students write about their own experiences
- A resources section listing helpful websites, publications and organisations

Free to download

Printed copies £3.99

"A great resource focused on the needs of disabled learners. The case studies are extremely useful, providing an insight into applying to and progressing through university. Highly recommended."

Undergraduate Recruitment and Widening Participation Coordinator, University of Manchester

You can buy our publications online at www.disabilityrightsuk.org

ON THE JOB LEARNING

The skills and learning that help your career most are often those you gain on the job. Of course, it's important to get good basic skills (like literacy and numeracy) and technical and educational qualifications but employers look for workplace skills, the skills to do the actual job, and 'softer' skills like teamwork, problem solving and customer service.

Jane Forster is a cashier with Barclays bank. "My optician noticed abnormalities at the back of my retina when I was 15 years old which was scary but also something of a relief. It meant I was finally taken seriously about problems I'd been having with my sight. Eventually I was diagnosed with Stargardt's Disease.

I had help and support from a charity called Henshaws Society for Blind People. They helped me on the road to employment with their Skillstep course. I learned CV writing, interview skills, basic word processing and other topics that help build up the skills you might need for work. I'm now doing an apprenticeship in Financial Services, an NVQ level 2 equivalent qualification. I chose Barclays as I thought it would be a good opportunity to work for a large company, especially having a disability.

That is one reason why apprenticeships, work experience and internships are growth areas.

You may find you get qualifications before working – but equally you may throw yourself into paid work, develop skills as you go, perhaps do training or qualifications later. There is no set pattern. So think creatively.

I also thought it would be interesting working in a bank.

Having a disability impacted on my training at first as there were delays waiting for equipment and adjustments to computer screens. I was a little disheartened but I decided to deal with it patiently. The training provider Elmfield and Barclays were very supportive throughout. I now have ZoomText software to enlarge the text on my computer. I also have an electronic magnifier and an audio PIN Sentry device to give the secure code needed for identifying customers. All of these have been provided by Barclays. My colleagues have also been extremely supportive, for example on the occasions when my equipment has failed. I've also had help and advice from friends, family, my Elmfield trainer and my line manager.

My experience has been very positive as I've realised I can overcome the barriers to working independently. My advice to others in a similar situation would be "Don't think you can't do the job because you've got a disability".

Brother and sister, Brett and Jessica Senior, started their first permanent jobs within days of each other.

Jessica, 19, is working as a receptionist and admin assistant at Express Coatings, following a two month work placement at the Sheffield firm. She has a visual impairment caused by the genetic condition Retinitis Pigmentosa and received support from Remploy's Sheffield branch.

Brett, who also has Retinitis Pigmentosa, had been unemployed for two years after leaving college. The 21-year-old, who registered with Remploy on his sister's recommendation, is now working as an assembly operator for confectionary maker Cadbury Trebor Bassett in Sheffield.

Brett and Jessica both received support from Remploy with job searching skills including writing an effective CV, interview techniques confidence building.

"My confidence was low when I first registered with Remploy but the help I received gave me self-belief", says Jessica, who is now working towards an NVQ Level 3 in Business Administration.

Brett adds: "Being unemployed for so long was no fun, so it's fantastic to have a job at last. I've met lots of new people and already made some good friends."

EMPLOYMENT SERVICES
The Work Programme
The Work Programme is a government employment programme, delivered by organisations contracted to do the work. It is designed to give personalised support to people who need more help looking for and staying in work.

Work Choice
Work Choice is a government employment programme designed for people who, due to their disability, may find it difficult to find or keep a job. Work Choice aims to identify your needs and provide the necessary support.

You may qualify if your disability means that you face significant barriers to work.

In addition you may have:
- complex work-related support needs
- requirements that can't immediately be overcome through workplace adjustments
- a need for support in work as well as help finding work.

If you have a complaint about a Work Programme provider or are unhappy with the service you have received, you should complain to them first and give them a chance to put the matter right. If you are unhappy with their response they must tell you how you can take your complaint further. If you are not satisfied with their final response, you can ask the Independent Case Examiner to investigate your complaint.
- Ⓦ www.gov.uk/government/organisations/independent-case-examiner

Disability Employment Advisors

A Disability Employment Adviser at your local Jobcentre can help you find a job or gain new skills and tell you about disability friendly employers in your area.

They can also refer you to a specialist work psychologist or carry out an 'employment assessment', asking you about your skills and experience and what kind of roles you're interested in.

Peer support

If you are worried about your job chances or generally lacking in confidence, find out as much as you can about people with health conditions and disabilities who are working in similar jobs or sectors.

Peer support services are run by many organisations, enabling people to learn and gain confidence from others. Specific employment peer support services are provided by people with experience of health conditions and disabilities – for example, Leeds Mind's Employment Peer Support Service or the programme run by Essex Coalition of Disabled People (ecdp) in Essex.

Such services can offer:

- a professional service that delivers the support that you want
- reliable and accurate information, advice and guidance
- strict confidentiality
- a supportive and understanding service
- signposting to other organisations where appropriate.

They can support you to find work by:

- developing an agreed action plan
- accessing internal and external training or work experience to gain necessary skills
- helping with CV preparation, job searching, application forms, interview preparation and contacting employers
- providing support with everyday issues that may be preventing you from working.

The power of peer support

Manchester-based disabled people's organisation, Breakthrough UK, offers personalised employment support: "We'll work with you, not make decisions for you". Support is designed around the client's own employment goals and needs. It is delivered by people with lived experience of the barriers of prejudice, environment and lack of support. Policy and practice is based on the social model of disability and clients learn to understand how barriers can be removed to enable them to work in any role or workplace.

Breakthrough UK also has a 'Talent Match' coach to work specifically with young people with disabilities and health conditions who have not been in employment, education or training for 12 months or over. They help them develop their personal and vocational skills and find apprenticeships, vocational training, work experience or volunteering on their journey to employment.
 ⓦ www.breakthrough-uk.co.uk

Progressing at work

Very senior people with disabilities and health conditions exist – as board level directors, departmental directors, non-executives and more. In 2010, Disability Rights UK conducted the first ever national survey of their experiences and found a significant senior talent pool of people with health conditions or disabilities who are 'flying high'.

Ⓦ www.disabilityrightsuk.org/doing-seniority-differently-summary

As a disabled person, I know about low expectations; about caring systems that sap ambition. But it is changing. Some of us are stripping away low expectations – and flying high. And some organisations are getting very serious about spotting and developing all the talents – which makes them more competitive as well as benefiting talented disabled people.

Phil Friend OBE, Chair, Disability Rights UK (2012-15)

> Baroness Campbell said: "Most reports on our experiences as disabled people focus on the barriers and problems we face. But if we focus first on problems, we often forget what is possible – we become pessimists. For me as a disabled member of the House of Lords I know it was my dreams that took me there, and the inspiration of others who had gone before me. That hope and optimism gave me the motivation to overcome the barriers in my path. If I had thought mainly about the barriers (and heaven knows there were many of them) I would have given up long ago."

Talking about your health or disability

People with a health condition or disability often wonder whether they should tell their employer, especially if it is not obvious. It's your choice whether and when you talk to people about your health or disability.

Think about the advantages of being open (like getting the support you need, feeling 'yourself', freedom from the energy sapping experience of keeping secrets).

Think about the potential downsides – might people see you differently, under-estimate you, 'kill you with kindness'? Presenting solutions and strategies helps others feel the issue is manageable. This can include talking about equipment that helps, other types of management and external support and any Access to Work package you have or expect to have.

> A Partner in the finance and accountancy sector said: "I have bi-polar mood disorder. The culture of the organisation helped me progress. It's a meritocracy here. And it is and always has been a very caring place – it's just the way you're brought up in the firm.
>
> I was open about my condition because that was the way to get help and understanding. Someone to open up to was a big part of what helped – and it's now in the manager's job description to support me in that way …. I definitely haven't been held back."

WHAT CAN MY EMPLOYER ASK ME?

Under the Equality Act 2010, an employer cannot normally ask you anything about your health or disability history until after they have made a job offer. This means that they cannot turn you down on health grounds without your knowledge.

However, employers can ask you before a job offer in limited circumstances, that is, if it is directly relevant to one of the following:

- whether you can take part in an assessment
- whether reasonable adjustments need to be made to a selection process
- whether you can carry out a task that is an essential part of the work
- as part of diversity monitoring among their job applicants
- to increase the number of disabled people they employ
- if disability is a requirement of the job
- national security checks.

If you think a question you are asked is not allowed before you have been offered a job, tell the employer and/or the Equality and Human Rights Commission.

Once you have been offered a job, the employer may ask for more information. However, the Equality Act still applies and this information cannot be used to discriminate in any way.

Bi-polar disorder often goes with creativity. That's a gift. But you have to learn how to manage that gift too.

WHAT DO I HAVE TO TELL MY EMPLOYER?

Under health and safety rules, you do have a legal obligation to tell your employer about any health condition that might cause an accident or other health and safety problem.

But apart from that, it's very much a personal choice and will depend on what your job is, your relationship with your employers and colleagues and their attitudes.

Present solutions

"The reason they gave me the job was that I said up-front at interview, 'You may think I can't cope, but I've thought it through. If you're worried about me using the blackboard, I can use an overhead projector instead – I'll buy my own if necessary.

I very much think, if you're disabled, it's your job to put other people at ease with you, because they don't know how to cope. You have to have confidence, put in the effort, and be candid. I think I've developed that confidence by necessity – it's not a natural thing. I just felt I wouldn't get anywhere if I sat back and let things happen.

The challenges posed by my disability mean colleagues see me as adaptable and resourceful.

Most people with disabilities have extra coping skills ... Sell those. It sets you apart from the herd."

One point to bear in mind is that your employer cannot make workplace adjustments if they do not know that any are required. Some actions which might be considered unfair if your employer knows about your disability or health condition may not be if they are unaware of it.

This debate may sound like something that only concerns people with invisible conditions but even those with obvious physical impairments need to think about how and when they might talk about them. This is important in the context of going to interviews or for promotion but is also relevant to your everyday working life.

Taking charge

Set your own expectations
If you decide to be open, think about who to talk to, when and how: just saying 'by the way I have bipolar or cancer' is very different from saying "I have bipolar and I've managed it successfully at work for some years now – and this is what would be helpful to me in my work, so I continue to work to my best".

You need to determine the nature of your relationship with your interviewer. Being disabled, people often don't know how to respond to you, how to treat you.

It's your job more than theirs to put things at ease, to be open about things and to determine how things are going to go.

If you have a fluctuating condition(s) with good days and bad days you'll perhaps choose to inform your colleagues and line manager in greater detail than those with a more fixed condition. If you have a degenerating condition, the question of what it is appropriate to say and when may well recur and you might find yourself returning to the questions in this section.

Staying in work after the onset of a health condition or disability

Of the working-age people with health conditions and disabilities in the UK, almost half are employed – but this figure should be higher. With the right support, many more could be in work – and keeping your job when you become disabled is crucial to this.

How employers can help disabled people stay in work

Trade unions can often provide support with retention. Dave Parr is a project worker with Disability Champions at Work, a TUC-backed organisation. He says that stereotypes about people with health conditions and disabilities can be the biggest work barrier. "The way to stop this is to educate people." If you're disabled or become disabled while in work, your employer should help you to stay in your job. Changes that your employer should consider – in consultation with you – include:
- transferring you to another post
- making changes to your place of work
- providing a reader or interpreter.

If you have recently developed a health condition or disability, you may be off work initially and/or worried about whether you will be able to stay in your job – or employment at all. The evidence shows that, sometimes with a period of time for readjustment, people with all types and degrees of severity of conditions and disabilities can and do work.

Getting the support you need
"Now, if I'm 'going off' I just stay at home and go through my recovery routine – two or three days – then come back and a colleague covers the work while I'm away. People understand this is what I need to do and completely accept it."

There's lots of guidance, support and training to help people into employment but less focussed on keeping people in work. This is a shame because staying with your existing employer, whether in the same or a new role, or returning to your own employer after a period of leave, offers the best chance of staying in work.

"I know my cancer could come back so while I don't work so hard as to make this more likely, I try to make sure that when I am working I opt for reasonably well-paid work that fits in with my values and beliefs rather than necessarily the most interesting work.

Volunteering to benefit others
Volunteering doesn't just benefit you. Many people with health conditions and disabilities are highly skilled and have worked in a wide variety of fields and sectors, or may have been responsible for organising activities for others in their family or local community.

A range of organisations in the UK promote volunteering as a powerful force for change, both for those who volunteer and for the wider community. Between them they have hundreds of thousands of volunteering opportunities.

These include:

Volunteering England
ⓦ www.volunteering.org.uk

Volunteers Scotland
ⓦ www.volunteerscotland.org.uk

Volunteering Wales
ⓦ www.volunteering-wales.net

Volunteering Northern Ireland
ⓦ www.volunteeringni.org

Information can also be found on the national volunteering database:
ⓦ www.do-it.org.uk

and through
ⓦ www.gov.uk

Britain's largest volunteer organisation CSV – provides opportunities for people with disabilities and learning difficulties to take part in a number of its projects.
ⓦ www.csv.org.uk

Voluntary work should not affect benefits so long as it genuinely is voluntary work (rather than, for example, helping out the family business) and the only money you receive is to cover your actual volunteering expenses. However, if you have any doubts, check before making any regular commitment.

The Department for Work and Pensions publish a booklet called *Volunteering while getting benefits*:
Ⓦ www.dwp.gov.uk/docs/dwp1023.pdf

Volunteering England has specific guidance for volunteers with disabilities and health conditions:
Ⓦ www.volunteering.org.uk/ component/gpb/disabled-people

In 2014 Disability Rights UK, with Community Service Volunteers and the Disability Action Alliance, launched a Volunteer Charter designed to help organisations welcome and be accessible to disabled volunteers.
Ⓦ http://disabilityrightsuk.org/ news/2014/december/volunteer-charter-launched

The Grace Eyre Foundation gives people 'structure and responsibility' and its volunteers range from those on the autistic spectrum and learning disabilities to those who are deaf. "Our volunteers are a mixed bag, a diverse range of people. For our travel buddies we have volunteers who have learning disabilities who act as buddies. They often know more about the bus routes than many other people would."

Leadership

There are many ways in which disabled people can take a lead in their community, profession, sector or country, such as being a charity trustee or on the board of a hospital or school, getting involved in a local community group. For example, Sadaqat Ali, who took part in Disability Rights UK's leadership programme, set up the first BSL signed service at a London Mosque.

For information about Disability Rights UK's leadership programme visit:
Ⓦ www.disabilityrightsuk.org/how-we-can-help/leadership

Marzia Sayani MBE, a leadership programme graduate said: "Since being awarded the MBE I have become a trustee of Milton Keynes Carers Group and Carers Bucks and a Member on the Carers Forum Group ... This is all due to [Disability Rights UK], as I really feel confident that I can take all that on board. A big thank you."

Having non-executive positions is a good way of stepping over the parapet. Broadening out your CV and experience, making sure you're not only sucked in to one thing. Often because of mobility issues, disabled people have narrower experiences, so the non-executive positions and appointments are a way of combating that.

Your rights
EQUALITY ACT 2010
Education and training

Your right to education is protected by the Equality Act 2010, which prohibits discrimination by governing bodies, schools, institutions of further and higher education and general qualifications bodies.

The Act means it is against the law for a school or other education provider to discriminate against you, harass you or victimise you because of your disability.

Schools, colleges, universities and any other education provider must make 'reasonable adjustments' to ensure disabled students are not discriminated against. These changes could include:

- providing extra support and aids (such as specialist teachers or equipment)
- changes to physical features to make the environment fully accessible.

To find out more about your rights as a disabled student in further or higher education:
- Ⓦ www.equalityhumanrights.com/ your-rights/service-users/education

Employment

The Equality Act 2010 also protects your rights in employment.

To help you understand the protection you have in employment, the Equality and Human Rights Commission has produced a series of guides on a wide range of subjects.

These include:

- Recruitment
- Working hours, flexible working and time off, pay and benefits
- Career development
- Management issues
- Dismissal, redundancy, retirement and after a worker has left
- Pre-employment health questionnaires
- Reasonable adjustments and removing barriers to work
- What to do if you've been discriminated against
- Equal pay.

Available from:
Ⓦ www.equalityhumanrights.com

UN CONVENTION ON THE RIGHTS OF PERSONS WITH DISABILITIES

Your rights to education, learning and employment are protected by this convention:
Ⓦ www.un.org/disabilities/convention/ conventionfull.shtml

Article 24 recognises your right to education and lifelong learning without discrimination.

It outlines your right to develop your full potential, including your creativity, mental and physical talents and abilities.

It says that the government must ensure that people with disabilities are not excluded from the education system on the basis of their disability, and that you must be able to access inclusive, quality, free primary and secondary education.

All education providers must make reasonable adjustments to accommodate your individual needs, with the right kind of support. They must make sure the learning environment is inclusive and gives you the best opportunity for academic and social development.

All staff should be trained in disability awareness, alternative means of communication, and techniques and materials to support your education.

You have the right to access further, higher or adult education, vocational training and lifelong learning without discrimination and reasonable accommodation must be provided.

Just as your right to education is protected by law, so is your right to employment.

Article 27 of the United Nations Convention for the Rights of Disabled Persons recognises your right to work on an equal basis with others, including your right to a fair, open and inclusive jobs market.

It also:
- prohibits discrimination on the basis of disability in recruitment, continuing employment, career advancement and safe and healthy working conditions
- protects your right to favourable work conditions, equal opportunities and pay, including protection from harassment, and the redress of grievances
- protects your right to be a member of a trade union on an equal basis with others
- protects your right to training at work
- promotes employment opportunities as well as assistance returning to work
- promotes opportunities for self-employment and entrepreneurship.

Leisure

Whether we like travel or photography, swimming or cinema, or we want to volunteer in our local area, we are entitled to facilities and support that enable us to take part.

This chapter provides information about a selection of organisations, activities and places that may be of interest. It's the tip of the iceberg, of course, there will be many more.

Getting involved

Being part of a community and developing friendships, skills and interests away from work or your home is an important part of leading an active and fulfilling life.

There are opportunities to take part in a wide range of activities depending on your interests. It's possible to take part in most activities that others enjoy, perhaps just with some adapted equipment or a change in activity times or environment.

It's easy to get a bit isolated when you are living with a disability or health condition. If you've had an operation or a recent diagnosis, and you're not feeling confident about new things, try going with someone the first time, or think through whether and how you want to mention what you're going through to get support.

Choosing your activity

You may already be engaged in hobbies, sport or community activities. But if the onset of a health condition or disability has made you reconsider what you can do, remember that people with similar challenges enjoy all sorts of activities.

A local library and the internet are good places to find ideas and information. Organisations in your area may be able to put you in touch with special interest groups – for example riding for disabled people or bowls for people with visual impairments – if you need substantial support.

Reading

Enjoying books can be difficult for some of us who, for whatever reason, cannot use or have difficulty with printed material. Audio books, newspapers and magazines are increasingly available in libraries and bookshops and through a tablet, mobile device, personal computer or e-reader.

The organisations below may also be able to help.

Bag Books
1 Stewart's Court, 218-220 Stewart's Road, London SW8 4UB
☎ 020 7627 0444
✉ office@bagbooks.org
🌐 www.bagbooks.org
Bag Books produces multi-sensory story packs for people with profound learning disabilities. Originally designed for children, the range now includes titles suitable for teenagers and adults.

Calibre Audio Library
Aylesbury HP22 5XQ
☎ 01296 43 2339
✉ enquiries@calibre.org.uk
🌐 www.calibre.org.uk
Calibre, a national charity, has a wide range of unabridged books on cassette or MP3 disc for adults and children who are visually impaired or cannot use printed books. Members can order items to borrow either by post or on the internet.

ClearVision
Linden Lodge School, 61 Princes Way, London SW19 6JB
☎ 020 8789 9575
🌐 www.clearvisionproject.org
ClearVision provides mainstream children's books incorporating Braille, print and pictures that can be shared by visually impaired children and sighted children and adults. Over 13,000 books are available. They are suitable for children learning Braille, or who may do so in the future, but not for partially sighted children learning to read print. Membership is free to families.

Assistive technology
Assistive technology is the general term used to describe the wide range of software and hardware designed to help disabled people with everyday tasks. Technical devices can be used to enable reading, including for people with visual impairments and dyslexia.

AbilityNet produce a range of factsheets written by speciaist assessors and consultants. They provide detailed information on a wide range of assistive technology and are free to download from the *Information* section of their website:
🌐 www.abilitynet.org.uk/factsheets

Action for blind people has a range of factsheets for people with visual impairments. You can find them in the *Practical advice* section of the Resources area of their website.
🌐 www.actionforblindpeople.org.uk/resources/practical-advice

Isis Publishing Ltd
7 Centremead, Osney Mead, Oxford OX2 0ES
- **T** 0800 731 5637
- **E** sales@isis-publishing.co.uk
- **W** www.isis-publishing.co.uk

Isis is a major audio publisher of unabridged titles on cassette, CD and MP3 formats to direct and internet customers.

Listening Books
12 Lant Street, London SE1 1QH
- **T** 020 7407 9417
- **E** info@listening-books.org.uk
- **W** www.listening-books.org.uk

Listening Books offers an audio book service to people for whom holding a book, turning a page or reading in the usual way is not possible.

RNIB National Library Service
PO Box 173, Peterborough PE2 6WS
- **T** 0303 123 9999
- **E** library@rnib.org.uk
- **W** www.rnib.org.uk

The Library Service aims to ensure that visually impaired people have the same access to library facilities as sighted people. It offers a lending service with many titles available in large print and electronic form as well as more traditional aural and tactile formats.

Inclusive Technology provides communication aids and assistive technology for people with a physical disability, sensory impairment or learning difficulty. Their website includes articles explaining the options available:
- **W** www.inclusive.co.uk/articles

The Arts, theatre and music

You can get information on going to the theatre or a gig, visiting a museum or gallery from a wide range of organisations. Some of them are listed below. The internet, radio and local and national newspapers are also good sources of information.

DisabledGo provides online access guides including detailed information gathered by personal inspections around the UK at a wide range of entertainment venues, places to visit, restaurants and shops.
- **W** www.disabledgo.com

Arts Council of England
14 Great Peter Street, London SW1P 3NQ
- **T** 0845 300 6200;
  textphone 020 7973 6564
- **W** www.artscouncil.org.uk

The Arts Council is responsible for arts funding and development in England and provides information and advice to artists and arts organisations including specific information on access for disabled people.

Arts Council of Northern Ireland
77 Malone Road, Belfast BT9 6AQ
- **T** 028 9038 5200
- **E** info@artscouncil-ni.org
- **W** www.artscouncil-ni.org

Creative Scotland
Waverley Gate, 2-4 Waterloo Place, Edinburgh EH1 3EG
- **T** 0845 603 6000
- **E** enquiries@creativescotland.com
- **W** www.creativescotland.com

Arts Council of Wales

Bute Place, Cardiff CF10 5AL
- 0845 873 4900;
  textphone 029 2045 0123
- info@artswales.org.uk
- www.artswales.org

Artsline

c/o 21 Pine Court, Wood Lodge Gardens,
Bromley BR1 2WA
- 020 7388 2227 (also textphone)
- www.artsline.org.uk

Artsline provides online information for disabled people on arts and events and activities in and around London. Full access details for London arts and entertainment venues and events are provided.

Attitude is Everything

54 Chalton Street, London NW1 1HS
- 020 7383 7979
- www.attitudeiseverything.org.uk

This organisation works with audiences, artists and the music industry to improve deaf and disabled people's access to live music. It promotes a *Charter of Best Practice* to venues and festivals throughout the country.

Disabled Photographers' Society

37 Orchard Close, New Barn, Longfield, Kent DA3 7JP
- enquiries@disabledphotographers.co.uk
- www.disabledphotographers.co.uk

The Society provides information on how you can adapt cameras and other photographic equipment and has access to engineers who can help. It arranges an annual exhibition of members' work and organises occasional photographic holidays and events. They have links with mainstream photographic bodies.

English Heritage

English Heritage's aims to help people 'understand, value, care for and enjoy England's heritage'. Their online *Places to visit* tool gives details of over 400 historical and archaeological sites to visit and includes access information.
- www.english-heritage.org.uk

If you are interested in disability or social history, *Disability in Time and Place* reveals how our lives as people with disabilities and health conditions are integral to the heritage all around us. From leper chapels built in the 1100s to protests about accessibility in the 1980s, the built environment is inextricably linked to our stories, hidden and well-known. Some of the buildings mentioned are open to the public.

Read more in the *Discover the past* section of the English Heritage website. All the content has been translated into British Sign Language.
- www.english-heritage.org.uk

Music and the Deaf

The Media Centre, 7 Northumberland Street, Huddersfield HD1 1RL

Ⓣ 01484 48 3115;
textphone 01484 48 3117

Ⓦ www.matd.org.uk

Music and the Deaf helps deaf people of all ages access music and the performing arts. It provides talks, signed theatre performances and workshops. In West Yorkshire it runs after-school clubs and a Deaf Youth Orchestra. They also run training days and collaborative projects with orchestras, opera, theatre and dance companies, and is one of the five lead organisations in Sing-up, a project to promote singing in schools.

MAGIC Deaf Arts is a group of major museums and art galleries in London which provides events and facilities for deaf and hard-of-hearing visitors, including specialist tours and sign-language interpreters. Their website includes a calendar of events.
Ⓦ www.magicdeaf.org.uk

National Theatre

South Bank, London SE1 9PX

Ⓣ 020 7452 3000

Ⓔ access@nationaltheatre.org.uk

Ⓦ www.nationaltheatre.org.uk

The National Theatre aims to be accessible and welcoming to all. Its three auditoriums have allocated wheelchair spaces and assistance dogs are welcome. Blind and visually impaired people can attend audio-described performances and touch tours, and get synopses notes and cast lists on CD or in Braille. Deaf and hearing impaired people can attend captioned performances.

Nordoff Robbins

2 Lissenden Gardens, London NW5 1PQ

Ⓣ 020 7267 4496

Ⓔ musicservices@nordoff-robbins.org.uk

Ⓦ www.nordoff-robbins.org.uk

A national organisation that seeks to use the power of music to transform the lives of children and adults living with illness, disability, trauma or in isolation. Their trained practitioners work in a range of settings including music therapy, music and health projects and community music schemes as well as the organisation's own centres.

Shape

Deane House Studios, 27 Greenwood Place, London NW5 1LB

Ⓣ 020 7424 7330;
textphone 020 7424 7368

Ⓦ www.shapearts.org.uk

Shape offers a range of activities to enable disabled and deaf people to participate and enjoy arts and cultural activities, mainly in the London area. Shape Tickets is a service offering its members tickets, often at reduced prices, at venues throughout London coupled with access assistance and transport if required.

Signed Performances in Theatre (SPIT)

6 Thirlmere Drive, Lymm, Cheshire WA13 9PE

Ⓦ www.spit.org.uk

SPIT promotes BSL interpreted performances in mainstream theatre and provides a link between arts organisations and the Deaf community. Its website includes a directory of signed and captioned performances nationwide.

STAGETEXT

1st floor, 54 Commercial Street, London
E1 6LT

T 020 7377 0540;
textphone 020 7247 7801

W www.stagetext.org

STAGETEXT provides access to the theatre for deaf and hard-of-hearing people through captioning. The full text, together with character names, sound effects and off-stage noises, is shown on LED displays as the words are spoken or sung. Around 200 productions are captioned each year in over 80 venues across the UK. Information on forthcoming performances is given on its website.

VocalEyes

1st floor, 54 Commercial Street, London
E1 6LT

T 020 7375 1043

E enquiries@vocaleyes.co.uk

W www.vocaleyes.co.uk

VocalEyes is a national organisation established to provide audio descriptions for performances in the theatre. It now also works in museums, galleries and architectural heritage sites. A programme of forthcoming events is published in print, Braille and on tape as well as on their website.

Zinc Arts

Great Stony, High Street, Chipping Ongar, Essex CM5 0AD

T 01277 36 5626;
textphone 01277 36 5003

E info@zincarts.org.uk

W www.zincarts.org.uk.

Zinc Arts aims to advance and promote the creativity, culture and heritage of disabled people and other socially excluded groups in Essex and Hertfordshire. It arranges a wide range of programmes.

Cinemas

Cinemas are becoming more accessible to people with impaired mobility, hearing or sight. The wide scale development of new cinema buildings means improvements in physical access, with most screens in multiplexes having spaces for wheelchair users.

In addition, many cinemas are now equipped to show films with digital subtitles and audio description. Film and venue information can be found at:

W www.yourlocalcinema.com

If you are registered blind, get Personal Independence Payment, Disability Living Allowance or Attendance Allowance, the Cinema Exhibitors' Association (CEA) offers a card verifying entitlement to a free ticket for a person accompanying you to a UK cinema. There is a £6 admin charge and the card has to be renewed each year.

W www.ceacard.co.uk

T 023 9224 8545;
textphone 18001 023 9224 8545

Days out

While most modern tourist attractions should be able to cater for all of us, do check first if you have specific requirements. Sites with a conservation aim, including historic buildings, nature reserves, forests and industrial heritage displays, may have limited access for some of us. However, many organisations are working to improve facilities.

These organisations have specialist publications and websites about their facilities:

Cadw: Welsh Historic Monuments

Plas Carew, Unit 5/7 Cefn Coed, Parc Nantgarw, Cardiff CF15 7QQ

T 01443 33 6000
E cadw@wales.gsi.gov.uk
W cadw.wales.gov.uk

English Heritage

Customer Services Department, Kemble Drive, PO Box 567, Swindon SN2 2YP

T 0870 333 1181;
  textphone 0800 015 0516
E customers@english-heritage.org.uk
W www.english-heritage.org.uk

The National Trust issues 'Access for All Admit One' (or Two) cards to admit a companion or carer of a disabled member free of charge. It's in the name of the disabled person, so you don't need to take the same companion on each visit. To request a card, call or email the National Trust Supporter Service Centre.

T 01793 817634
E enquiries@nationaltrust.org.uk

Historic Scotland

Longmore House, Salisbury Place, Edinburgh EH9 1SH

T 0131 668 8600
W www.historic-scotland.gov.uk

National Trust

The National Trust Supported Centre, PO Box 574, Manvers, Rotherham, S63 3FH

T 01793 817 400
E enquiries@nationaltrust.org.uk
W www.nationaltrust.org.uk

National Trust for Scotland

Hermiston Quay, 5 Cultins Road, Edinburgh EH11 4DF

T 0131 458 0303
E information@nts.org.uk
W www.nts.org.uk

Royal Society for the Protection of Birds

The Lodge, Potton Road, Sandy, Bedfordshire SG19 2DL

T 01767 68 0551
W www.rspb.org.uk

Shopping

While some people find going to the shops a chore, for others going shopping or looking round the shops is a fun activity. The growth of purpose-built shopping centres has made things easier for many of us.

Shopmobility

Shopmobility schemes provide wheelchairs and scooters for hire and use in many shopping centres throughout the UK. Some schemes provide children's wheelchairs, escorts or special services for people visiting their area.

You can find your nearest Shopmobility scheme in their online directory. You'll need to contact a specific scheme to make equipment bookings or find out detailed information.

National Federation of Shopmobility
PO Box 6641, Christchurch BH23 9DQ
☎ 0844 414 1850
✉ info@shopmobilityuk.org
🌐 www.shopmobilityuk.org

Adult education
You may want to learn more about a subject for your own personal interest or to gain vocational skills.

Schools, colleges (including specialist adult education centres) and other community facilities offer day and evening courses. Most adult courses are organised by adult education colleges but there are a variety of other providers including university extra-mural departments. They should be accessible to you.

There have been courses specifically for students with disabilities and health conditions for a long time. However, it is increasingly possible to join mainstream courses. Prospectuses provide basic information and a named contact if you want to know more.

Adult Residential Colleges Association (ARCA)
6 Bath Road, Felixstowe IP11 7JW
🌐 www.arca.uk.net
This association of small colleges specialises in short-stay residential courses for the general public. Each college has its own programme of weekend, midweek and day courses, and some offer summer schools and courses leading to recognised qualifications. A range of accommodation is available and most dietary needs can be catered for. Many of the colleges have facilities for disabled people. Check individual requirements before booking.

University of the Third Age (U3A)
Old Municipal Buildings, 19 East Street, Bromley BR1 1QE
☎ 020 8466 6139
🌐 www.u3a.org.uk
U3A promotes autonomous local learning groups for people no longer in full-time employment. Local groups are run by volunteers and operate as learning cooperatives which draw upon their member's knowledge, experience and skills to organise and provide educational, creative and leisure opportunities There are almost 750 independent local U3A groups in the UK with over 259,000 members.

Workers' Educational Association (WEA)
4 Luke Street, London EC2A 4XW
☎ 020 7426 3450
✉ national@wea.org.uk
🌐 www.wea.org.uk
The WEA is a major national voluntary adult education organisation providing over 10,000 courses a year, mainly arranged through local branches.

Around the UK contact:

WEA Northern Ireland
3 Fitzwilliam Street, Belfast BT9 6AW
☎ 028 9032 9718
🌐 www.wea-ni.com

WEA Scottish Association
Riddles Court, 322 Lawnmarket, Edinburgh EH1 2PG
☎ 0131 226 3456
✉ hq@weascotland.org.uk
🌐 www.weascotland.org.uk

WEA South Wales
7 Coopers Yard, Curren Road, Cardiff CF10 5NB
☎ 029 2023 5277
✉ weasw@weasouthwales.org.uk
🌐 www.weasouthwales.org.uk

WEA North Wales
Coleg Harlech, Harlech, Gwynedd LL46 2PU
☎ 01766 78 1900 (Residential courses)
01248 35 3254 (Community courses)
🌐 www.harlech.ac.uk

Fitness and sport

The growing success and recognition of the UK's Paralympians is a powerful reminder that physical activity is for everyone. It does not have to be competitive or at such a demanding level. Simply getting more active will bring important health benefits and can help you manage daily life. There are social benefits too – exercise helps you get out, meet people and make friends.

Exercise boosts mood and energy levels and improves sleep. It's believed to help memory and brain function and to reduce stress.

Whatever your preferences and level of physical ability, there will be options to suit you.

The NHS is a good starting point for information on the benefits of an active life. Visit the *Live Well* section of the NHS Choices website to find information on:
• general fitness
• keeping fit with a disability
• physical activity for wheelchair users
• exercise and disability
• find health and wellbeing services near you
• exercise you can do at home.

Disability Rights UK's guide *Doing Sport Differently* is a comprehensive guide to accessing sporting and physical activities. Sponsored by VISA, the guide covers a wide range of sport and fitness activities from rambling to archery. To download a copy visit:
🌐 www.disabilityrightsuk.org

Sport England

Sport England supports sport for everyone, helping to make sure everyone has access to high quality facilities. They recognise that only one in six people with a disability or health condition play sport regularly, compared to one in three non-disabled people. They aim to enable people with disabilities and health conditions to view taking part in exercise and sport as a realistic lifestyle choice. You may be eligible for funding to help with buying sports equipment or improving disabled sports facilities.

Ⓦ www.sportengland.org/our-work/disability

The English Federation of Disability Sport, in partnership with Disability Rights UK, has published *Being Active, an everyday guide for people living with an impairment or health condition.* The guide aims to increase the number of disabled people choosing to lead an active lifestyle. It gives inactive disabled people access to relevant information so they have control over where, what and how they can start being active. You can download a copy from the *Resources* section of their website.

Ⓦ www.efds.co.uk

English Federation of Disability Sport

The English Federation of Disability Sport is the national body dedicated to activity and sport for people with disabilities and health conditions throughout England.

Its website includes links to:
- inclusive gyms across England
- sports in your area
- jobs in sport
- links to other disabled sports organisations.

SportPark, Loughborough University, 3 Oakwood Drive, Loughborough, Leicestershire LE11 3QF

Ⓣ 01509 227750
Ⓦ www.efds.co.uk

There are equivalent organisations in Scotland, Wales and Northern Ireland.

Scottish Disability Sport

Caledonia House, South Gyle, Edinburgh EH12 9DQ

Ⓣ 0131 317 1130
Ⓔ admin@scottishdisabilitysport.com
Ⓦ www.scottishdisabilitysport.com

Disability Sport Northern Ireland

Adelaide House, Falcon Road, Belfast BT12 6SJ

Ⓣ 028 9038 7062; textphone 028 9038 7064
Ⓦ www.dsni.co.uk

Disability Sport Wales

Sport Wales National Centre, Sophia Gardens, Cardiff CF11 9SW

Ⓣ 0845 846 0021
Ⓦ www.disabilitysportwales.com

British Paralympics Association (BPA)
60 Charlotte Street, London W1T 2NU
T 020 7842 5789
E info@paralympics.org.uk
W www.paralympics.org.uk
Aside from being the representative organisation for elite Paralympians, the BPA also provides Parasport, which has been designed to inspire, educate, inform and signpost disabled people, and those interested in disability sport, to high-quality opportunities. Parasport aims to help us find our personal best. You can access it via the website.

Be Inspired has an online database giving details of thousands of public and private sports facilities in England including activities available, charges, membership and accessibility for disabled people.
W www.beinspireduk.org

The Time to Change campaign, which tackles mental health discrimination, has a range of resources about getting active when you have a mental health condition.
W www.time-to-change.org.uk

Staying healthy
"I have a number of health conditions – including diabetes and depression. I find walking regularly on my own or with other people makes a massive difference. It gets me outside. It gets the endorphins going. It's helping me to maintain a healthy weight – something I struggled with before."

ADAPTED ACTIVITIES
Many games can be played by people with disabilities and health conditions on the same basis as non-disabled people. Some have also been adapted to make them more disability-friendly. Some adaptations are slight, others more significant. For example, football for people with learning disabilities is played by the same rules, as is deaf football – except referees use flags rather than whistles. 'Blind football' is five-a-side with sighted goalkeepers, a ball filled with ball bearings and no offside rule.
W www.disabilityfootball.co.uk

SPECTATOR FACILITIES
The creation of new and enlarged stadia, greater awareness of our access needs and the impact of regulations means improved facilities for spectators in many places. At many football grounds, for example, audio commentary is available for visually impaired supporters and many race courses now have raised platforms for wheelchair users.

There are still limitations so it is always worth contacting venues in advance to find out about accessible facilities or to ask about a particular facility or service.

Event Mobility Charitable Trust
8 Bayliss Road, Kemerton, Tewkesbury
GL20 7JH
☎ 01386 72 5391
✉ info@eventmobility.org.uk
🌐 www.eventmobility.org.uk
Some events are problematic for us
to attend because they extend over a
large area or the facilities for spectators
are temporary. Event Mobility hires out
powered scooters and wheelchairs at
a range of events including agricultural
and countryside shows, major golf
championships and horse shows.
Bookings need to be made in advance.
Visit the website for a list of events or to
make a booking.

Access information
Access information for many venues
is available from Level Playing Field
(LPF), an organisation dedicated to
disabled sports fans.

LPF is a charity operating in England
and Wales. It acts as a campaigning
and advisory organisation to its
membership and other parties
across all sports.

On its website, you will find
information on disabled fans
facilities at clubs and stadia, along
with football, disability and access
reports, guides, good practice
documents and general disabled
supporter information.

You'll also find the latest news items
and a back catalogue of the Level
Playing Field e-newsletters.
🌐 www.levelplayingfield.org.uk

Sportsable
Braywick Sports Ground, Maidenhead
SL6 1BN
☎ 01628 62 7690
✉ info@sportsable.co.uk
🌐 www.sportsable.co.uk
Promotes awareness of disability through
sport and encourages integration of
disabled and non-disabled people. They
run a sports club providing facilities for
disabled people in Maidenhead. They
also introduce sport to disabled people
in the community through outreach
programmes with schools and clubs.

SPECIFIC SPORTING ACTIVITIES
These are just some of the organisations
and projects concerned with helping us
take part in specific sporting activities.

**British Disabled Angling Association
(BDAA)**
9 Yew Tree Road, Delves, Walsall WS5
4NQ
☎ 01922 86 0912
🌐 www.bdaa.co.uk
Represents disabled anglers across the
UK, including coarse, sea, specimen and
game fishing. Services include: courses,
group development, access audits of
fishing areas, training people to coach
disabled people and disability awareness
training.

Disability Snowsport UK
Glenmore Grounds, Aviemore PH22 1RB
☎ 01479 86 1272
✉ admin@disabilitysnowsport.org.uk
🌐 www.disabilitysnowsport.org.uk
Offers ski instruction at a purpose-built
adaptive ski school at Cairngorm and at
ski slopes around the country. Activity
weeks are held in Europe and America.

Inclusive Fitness Initiative (IFI)

Sport Park, Loughborough University, 3 Oakwood Drive, Loughborough LE11 3QF

- **T** 01509 22 7750
- **E** ifi@efds.co.uk
- **W** www.efds.co.uk

Launched by the English Federation for Disability Sport, IFI promotes the provision and management of integrated facilities for disabled people in general fitness centres. It accredits venues that provide accessible facilities, inclusive fitness equipment, appropriate staff straining and inclusive marketing.

RYA Sailability

RYA House, Ensign Way, Hamble, Southampton SO31 4YA

- **T** 0844 556 9550
- **E** sailability@rya.org.uk
- **W** www.rya.org.uk/sailability

RYA Sailability promotes and co-ordinates participation by disabled people in the sailing community. It provides information to individuals on where they can sail and supports sailing centres and clubs in improving opportunities for disabled people.

A fisherman's tale

"I can't tell you the feeling of well-being it gives me to go flyfishing. I used to love sport – was into everything as a boy. When I broke my back, I just gave it all up. I spend so much of my time inside or in the car now. Being up at the crack of dawn, on the bank or in the wheelie-boat, it's amazing. It puts me close to nature. Close to myself. I love it."

Motorsport Endeavour

123 Ealing Village, London W5 2EB

- **T** 020 8991 2358
- **E** info@motorsportendeavour.com
- **W** www.motorsportendeavour.com

Motorsport Endeavour runs events involving disabled people in all forms of motorsport. A wide-ranging programme includes rallies, karting and visits to motorsport venues. The club is open to drivers as well as people wishing to take other roles such as navigators, marshals, timekeepers and spectators. Motorsport Endeavour is also establishing links for disabled people who are seeking employment in the motorsport industry.

Thrive

The Geoffrey Udall Centre, Beech Hill, Reading RG7 2AT

- **T** 0118 988 5688
- **E** info@thrive.org.uk
- **W** www.thrive.org.uk

Thrive aims to improve the lives of elderly and disabled people through gardening and horticulture. It runs demonstration gardens, supports a network of community and therapeutic gardening projects and runs training courses. It runs the Blind Gardeners' Club and produces publications and factsheets offering practical advice on many gardening topics. Their website (www.carryongardening.co.uk) provides information about equipment and techniques to make gardening easier. www.accessiblegardens.org.uk has a directory of gardens with accessibility reviews written by people with disabilities. The site also has articles about people, organisations and schools involved with gardens.

The Wheelyboat Trust
North Lodge, Burton Park, Petworth
GU28 0JT
☏ 01798 34 2222
✉ info@wheelyboats.org
🌐 www.wheelyboats.org
The Trust places specially designed
Wheelyboats on lakes and other waters
in all parts of the British Isles where they
can be used for fishing, bird-watching or
other activities. The boats have a bow
door which lowers to form a boarding
ramp and the open level deck provides
access throughout. For a list of locations,
ring or visit the website.

Further information
Organisations that promote specific
sports for people with a disability or
health needs:
- 🌐 www.britishblindsport.org.uk
- 🌐 www.britishjudo.org.uk
- 🌐 www.britishwheelchairsports.org
- 🌐 www.bewsa.org (British Ex-
  services Wheelchair Sports
  Association)
- 🌐 www.bwaa.co.uk (British
  Wheelchair Athletes Association)
- 🌐 www.disabilityfootball.co.uk
- 🌐 www.disabilitysnowsport.org.uk
- 🌐 www.disabilitysportscoach.co.uk
- 🌐 www.dsactive.org (Down's
  Syndrome Association)
- 🌐 www.iwasf.com (Wheelchair and
  Amputee Sports Federation)
- 🌐 www.mencap.org.uk (Mencap
  Sport)
- 🌐 www.motorsportendeavour.com
- 🌐 www.paralympics.org.uk
- 🌐 www.parasport.org.uk

Disabled Ramblers Association
The Association helps mobility-
challenged people get back out into the
countryside. Non-disabled helpers are
welcome to support members and to
help with loading scooters and other
jobs.

Disabled ramblers ramble in all weathers
and over a variety of terrain. Rambles
are graded according to difficulty. Some
are suitable for shopping buggies and
power chairs whilst others need large
scooters capable of traveling over rough
ground.

Rambling and roaming
"Disabled ramblers have at least
one thing in common. We can't
walk sufficiently well to enjoy a day
out on foot but want to see views
and visit interesting places in the
countryside. Come on a ramble and
you will not feel out of place, with
friendly, like-minded people on an
informal, relaxed day."

The Association spends a lot of time
researching routes and working with the
authorities to improve access. Many of
its rambles are accompanied by staff
from the area. This adds to enjoyment
of the ramble through their local
knowledge and the extra security they
can often provide. About 30 rambles are
run each year across England and Wales
– mostly from March to October.

Let's Go Rambling is a comprehensive
insight into rambling with the
Association.
🌐 http://disabledramblers.co.uk

Accessible play for children

According to Play England, outdoor play is crucial for a child's development and wellbeing, and it must be made fully accessible to all.

A child's right to play is outlined by article 31 of the United Nations Convention on the Rights of the Child, but this right is often ignored. People often get particularly anxious about outdoor play.

> **A campaigner's tale**
> "We really had to fight it. My child is considered a health and safety risk when we try to go to soft play places and parks. I'm not having it. I want her to be as fit, healthy and confident physically as she can be. I use the law when I have to – with a smile on my face. That usually makes them back off. It's hard – but it's worth it to see my daughter's smile as she enjoys herself."

Outdoor play is essential to the healthy physical, social and emotional development of all children. It can be hugely stimulating and exciting and it offers unique opportunities for adventure, challenge and personal development.

Play England has a Love Outdoor Play campaign, which calls on everyone to support children's freedom to play outside. There are many ways to get involved and the campaign promotes a wide range of actions to ensure that anyone can be involved with outdoor play. The Cabinet Office's Social Action Fund is funding the campaign via the

Play England Free Time Consortium, a group of 17 organisations which aims to increase social action in support of children's play.
Ⓦ www.kids.org.uk

Information on Play England's Love Outdoor Play campaign can be found at:
Ⓦ www.loveoutdoorplay.net

Your rights
THE UN CONVENTION ON THE RIGHTS OF PERSONS WITH DISABILITIES

Your right to play an active part in your community, to participate in cultural or public life, recreation, leisure and sport, and to access opportunities and services is protected by the United Nations Convention on the Right of Persons with Disabilities.
Ⓦ www.un.org/disabilities/convention/conventionfull.shtml

Article 19 outlines your right to live independently and play a full and active part in your community.

Article 24 focuses on education and equal opportunity. It protects your right to learn the communication skills you need to fulfil your potential and participate in your community.

Article 30 protects your right to take part in cultural, leisure or sporting activities on an equal basis. This includes having full access to:

- cultural materials in accessible formats
- TV programmes, films, theatre and other cultural activities, in accessible formats
- theatres, museums, cinemas, libraries, tourism sites and services.

The Convention also safeguards your right to develop and use your creative, artistic and intellectual talents. It explains that you are entitled to have your cultural or language needs recognised and supported in the wider community through things like sign language.

THE EQUALITY ACT

The Equality Act 2010 enshrines your right to equality in the UK and gives you legal protection against discrimination. It outlines your rights in the way you use services, facilities or receive goods in your community.

The Equality and Human Rights Commission is a good source of information on how this legislation fully protects your rights:

- Ⓦ www.equalityhumanrights.com/your-rights/equal-rights/disability

Anyone who provides a service to the public, or a section of the public, is a service provider – and this includes leisure centres, swimming pools, ice rinks, banks, shops, theatres, galleries, museums, arts festivals, community venues or centres. If you are using sporting facilities, you should be able to change in the same comfort as a non-disabled person.

Providers need to make reasonable adjustments so you can use their services – if they don't they may be in breach of the law.

Asking for reasonable adjustments
Jade Peterson regularly goes with friends to a restaurant near her home. She has a visual impairment but is able to read print as long as it is at least 14 point.

Jade points out to the restaurant manager that many people would struggle to read the very small print on the menu and politely explains that the Equality Act requires providers of services to make reasonable changes to how they do things. The manager says that she will look into it and when Jade returns two weeks later a larger print menu is available.

YOUR CONSUMER RIGHTS

The Equality Act means you have the right to redress if you feel you have been discriminated against. You have the right to be a member of any club or association that a non-disabled person is allowed to join. Some private sports or special interest clubs with fewer than 25 members, however, can turn you down for membership in particular circumstances. But, whether or not an organisation is entitled to discriminate in this way is a question of law.

CONSUMER LAW

General consumer law also protects your consumer rights when you buy goods or services. You can get help if you're treated unfairly or when things go wrong. This includes:

- credit and store cards
- faulty goods
- counterfeit goods
- poor service
- problems with contracts
- problems with builders
- rogue traders.

For information about complaints, refunds and repairs:

Ⓦ www.which.co.uk/consumer-rights/
   action

Citizens Advice can give you advice about your consumer rights. They can also refer your complaint to local Trading Standards officers who will then investigate on your behalf.

Ⓦ www.adviceguide.org.uk/
   consumer_e.htm

You'll find information about making complaints in the chapter on your rights.

Special rights for disabled consumers
Jayne Knight says: "My Railcard has been a great asset to me and I feel that a lot more eligible people, who are, at the moment, rather wary of applying for a card could benefit if they saw how much more adventurous their lives could be.

My card is indispensible, giving me the freedom to travel about the land ... and I really would not have visited so many interesting places without it. I have just renewed my card ... and arranged a couple of days out involving rail journeys, so the 1/3 discount ... means I will have recouped part of the £54 layout immediately.

Another nice touch is that a travelling companion receives the same discount, which is very helpful to me as, with limited mobility, I depend on assistance.

It is also reassuring to find there is a designated wheelchair space reserved for me on the train (near an accessible loo!) and all the rail staff are helpful, attentive, polite and very kind at the stations and on board the trains".

Consultancy services

Would you like to reach more disabled customers, employ more disabled people and help your existing employees work to their full potential? We know that businesses that perform well for disabled customers and staff perform exceptionally for everyone.

What we can help you achieve

We provide bespoke disability knowledge and confidence training that can bring about measurable change for your organisation:

- What disability legislation means for your business
- Disability equality in the workplace and for your customers
- Disability awareness training
- Inclusive recruitment and HR practices
- Product or service evaluation through focus groups and user panels
- Management of health and wellbeing in the workplace

Our expertise

As an organisation which supports people with every type of disability or health condition, we have a unique perspective on the concerns, issues and aspirations of disabled people in the UK. We've worked successfully with public, private and voluntary sector organisations to help them deliver outstanding customer service, employment and HR practices. To find how we could help you email **jason.jaspal@disabilityrightsuk.org**

"We commissioned Disability Rights UK to help us understand disabled customer needs. The report contained a wealth of information that exceeded our expectations in terms of insight and value."

Programmes also delivered for:

www.disabilityrightsuk.org/how-we-can-help/consultancy

Your rights and discrimination

None of us should have to put up with unfair treatment. If we have a disability or health condition, organisations will be breaking the law if they discriminate against us.

The laws protecting people with disabilities and health conditions are relatively recent – the first was passed just under 20 years ago. It only happened because people like us campaigned long and hard for many years for equality in education, employment, transport and other areas of life such as buying things, joining clubs and using insurance and health services. We also have a range of human and consumer rights.

What is discrimination?

Discrimination can take a variety of forms. It is important that we recognise when we are being treated unfairly, can explain why it is wrong and take action to deal with it.

For example, if we experience any of these things it is likely that we are being discriminated against:

- teachers refuse to take a pupil on a school trip because they consider them more of 'a risk'
- a passenger explains to a bus driver that he will need to face her so that she can lipread what he says – but he refuses
- a customer arrives at a restaurant that has plenty of empty tables and a 'no booking policy' – but is told that the restaurant is full (they suspect it is because their speech is less distinct than most people's because they have cerebral palsy)

- an employee develops a heart condition and wants to move from full-time to part-time hours – but the business they work for won't agree
- an employee is suddenly made redundant after telling a colleague that they once experienced depression.

This is just a handful of possible ways in which people have been discriminated against. Sometimes it is put in terms of "it's better for you", sometimes "it's a risk to other people" or "it's too expensive".

All of these situations can be challenged and potentially resolved by explaining our rights and seeking support if we need to. Others have done so. We can too. And there are organisations that can help.

The importance of peer support

If you are facing discrimination, talk to someone you trust. Your local disabled people's organisation (DPO) may be able to support you in using your rights.

We all benefit from talking to someone who has a shared or similar experience and this is especially true if you have had a change in your health, circumstances or abilities and want to assert your rights but are not sure how.

Being able to talk to someone who is able to understand your concerns or questions can be very useful. This is called peer support and there are local organisations and community led groups across the country that you can get in touch with.

DPOs operate locally or nationally, and are run by people with health conditions and disabilities for people with health conditions and disabilities.

They differ in the services they offer. They will describe themselves in different ways, including as a centre for independent living.

Disability Rights UK and the UK Disabled People's Council are good places to begin finding a disabled people's organisation to meet your needs. Visit their websites for more information.
Ⓦ www.disabilityrightsuk.org
Ⓦ www.ukdpc.net/site

Am I 'disabled'?

Many people don't describe themselves as 'disabled', despite meeting the definitions used in the Equality Act to protect people from 'disability discrimination' or in the criteria for particular 'disabled benefits'.

This can be the case if they have a health condition or impairment that isn't visible. Conditions such as diabetes, dyslexia, hearing impairments, sleep disorders, chronic pain or arthritis can affect your everyday activities but they may not be obvious to other people.

You don't have to describe yourself as 'disabled' in everyday life but using this term in some contexts can be useful.

For example:
- you will need to be open about your disability if you want to claim your right to reasonable adjustments in school or at work
- you may be entitled to benefits such as Employment Support Allowance or Personal Independence Payment.

The decision about whether to tell others about a disability or health condition, particularly at work, can feel daunting. Many of us find that being open is liberating – we can be fully ourselves. But it's a personal decision.

The Equality Act 2010 is there to protect you from unfair discrimination if you decide to talk about it.

Equality Act

The Equality Act 2010 sets out your rights and explains how the law can protect you from discrimination. It offers protection to nine characteristics including disability.

The Act describes disability as a physical or mental impairment which has a substantial and long-term adverse effect on a person's ability to carry out normal day-to-day activities.

It sets out five forms of discrimination:
- direct discrimination
- indirect discrimination
- discrimination arising from disability
- failure to make reasonable adjustments
- harassment and victimisation.

Taking charge

Challenging discrimination

A school finds out that a pupil has been diagnosed as autistic and immediately excludes him from the school play as they think he will "not be able to cope". His mother points out that this is illegal – an example of direct discrimination. She does not immediately threaten legal action, is polite and gives them the opportunity to change their decision.

The school had thought they were acting in the pupil's interest but reconsider, give him a part in the play and provide training on the Equality Act and on autism for all staff. They invite the pupil and his mother to the school to discuss any adjustments that they can make.

If you know your rights you can use them to negotiate for what you need. For instance, if you are turned away from a café because you have an assistance dog with you, explaining the law and reassuring them that the dog is trained may change their practice – and their attitude for the next customer with an assistance dog.

The Equality and Human Rights Commission

The Equality and Human Rights Commission (EHRC) was set up by Parliament to help make Britain a fairer place for everyone. The Commission helps us secure our rights and eliminate discrimination through information, advice and, sometimes, support with legal cases.

The Commission has the power to make sure the law is working as intended. Beyond the Commission, there are many other organisations that can help and advise you if you are concerned that you have been treated unfairly. You'll find contacts for some of them at the end of this chapter.

For more information
You can find information about the Equality Act, the role of the Commission and guidance for individuals and organisations on the EHRC website.
ⓦ www.equalityhumanrights.com

Equality and Human Rights Commission

Adele's story

Adele Matthew used Article 3 of the European Convention on Human Rights Act (prohibition of torture, and inhuman or degrading treatment or punishment) in a landmark case regarding her treatment in police custody and in prison.

Due to damage by the drug Thalidomide, Adele was born with shortened arms and legs and uses a wheelchair. She also has kidney problems. She was sent to prison in 1995, after being taken to court over a debt. During the case, she refused to answer questions about her financial position, and was sentenced to seven days in custody for contempt of court.

As it was not possible to take Adele to prison until the next day, she spent the night at Lincoln Police Station. Her cell contained a wooden bed and a mattress. It was not adapted and as a result, she was forced to sleep in her wheelchair and was unable to use the toilet. The light switches and emergency buttons were out of her reach.

The police custody record showed that during the night, she complained of the cold every half hour (a serious problem for someone with recurring kidney problems). After she made several complaints, a doctor was called who noted Adele could not use the bed or leave her wheelchair. The doctor also said the cell was too cold and officers were told the facilities were not adapted to the needs of a disabled person. Despite the doctor's comments, no action was taken and Adele remained in the cell overnight.

The next day, Adele was moved to New Hall Women's Prison, Wakefield, and detained in the prison's health care centre until the afternoon of 23 January. Once again she had difficulty using the toilet in her cell and felt humiliated when male prison officers were required to lift her on and off the toilet. "I was sitting in my own faeces and urine in a wheelchair. No one should be made to go through that experience", she says.

By the time of her release, Adele was suffering from health problems which continued for ten weeks. On 30 January she consulted solicitors with a view to bringing an action in negligence against the Home Office.

On 10 July 2001, the European Court of Human Rights found in Adele's favour and said there had been a violation of Article 3. The court said that to detain a severely disabled person in conditions where she is dangerously cold, risks developing sores because her bed is too hard or unreachable, and is unable to go to the toilet or keep clean without the greatest of difficulty, constitutes degrading treatment. Adele says: "I try not to think about what happened because if I do I get very upset ... I was very pleased at the decision ... The Human Rights Act helped me and I hope it makes a huge difference for other disabled people".

UN Convention on the Rights of Persons with Disabilities

 International laws also protect your right to live without discrimination in an inclusive and fair society. This United Nations Convention protects people with disabilities 'including those who have long-term physical, mental, intellectual or sensory impairments which in interaction with various barriers may hinder their full and effective participation in society on an equal basis with others'. It spells out your right to fair treatment in your personal and home life, at school, work, and all aspects of society.

Ⓦ www.un.org/disabilities/convention/conventionfull.shtml

You'll find details of specific Convention rights in most chapters in this guide.

 Disability Rights UK has written a booklet on behalf of the EHRC about the UN Convention. *What does it mean for you?* can be found in the Private and public sector guidance section of the EHRC website.

Ⓦ www.equalityhumanrights.com

The Equality and Human Rights Commission, the Scottish Human Rights Commission, the Northern Ireland Human Rights Commission and the Northern Ireland Equality Commission have a responsibility to 'promote, protect and monitor implementation' of the Convention in the UK.

The Human Rights Act

The Human Rights Act 1998 came into force in the United Kingdom in October 2000. It is made up of a series of sections that codify the protections in the European Convention on Human Rights into UK law.

All public bodies (such as courts, police, local governments, hospitals, publicly funded schools, and others) and other bodies carrying out public functions have to comply with the Convention rights.

This means, among other things, that people can take human rights cases in domestic courts; they no longer have to go to Strasbourg to argue their case in the European Court of Human Rights.

Human rights in action

Equally Ours is a partnership between eight national charities who have come together to raise awareness of how the Human Rights Act benefit us all in everyday life.

They have lots of resources explaining what human rights mean in our everyday lives, for example:

Putting human rights at the heart of mental health care:

Ⓦ www.equally-ours.org.uk/putting-human-rights-heart-mental-health-care-2

When we need more help if we have a disability:

Ⓦ www.equally-ours.org.uk/need-help-disability

Catherine's story

In 2005, Catherine (not her real name) was raped by a stranger who she had invited into her home.

She has bi-polar disorder and on the day she was raped, she was experiencing a psychotic episode. "I thought it was the last judgment day and everyone had to look after each other. I made him a hot chocolate. He was asking me to kiss him and I said no. And then he moved me forcibly into the bedroom and I knew I was going to be raped", she says.

The day after the rape, Catherine was detained by the police when she was found stopping traffic, and sectioned under the Mental Health Act. It was from the hospital two months later, in December 2005, that she first reported the rape to police in her home town of Cambridge.

In February 2006, she contacted the police to find out how the investigation was progressing. She discovered that nothing at all had been done, and that her allegation had not been recorded as a crime. Catherine believes her mental illness played a part in the police's failure to investigate.

The man who raped Catherine has never been caught. When she discovered that footage showing her rapist forcing Catherine to take out money from a cashpoint had been lost, she decided to launch a formal complaint against the Cambridgeshire force.

An internal investigation began. The sergeant who let paperwork lie on his desk denied that he had ignored the case because the woman making the complaint had mental health problems. He was given a superintendent's written warning. The female officer who had initially dealt with Catherine received words of advice.

Catherine was still not satisfied with the police response. She found a solicitor who argued that there had been a breach of human rights law. Under Article 3 of the European Convention on Human Rights (prohibition of torture, and inhuman or degrading treatment or punishment), the state has a duty to investigate all cases where an individual has been subject to inhuman or degrading treatment.

After legal action began, Cambridgeshire Police settled out of court and paid Catherine £3,500 in compensation. The force admitted no liability but issued a letter of apology.

"This victory is important, since it can begin to address this attitude that the police have towards the vulnerable", Catherine says.

"The Human Rights Act holds the police to account. I see my legal victory not as an end but as a beginning and I want it to be a message to women and men who are disadvantaged – whether it is in terms of ethnicity, poverty, illness or disability – that they have legal rights and the state has obligations to fulfill these rights."

The Act sets out the fundamental rights and freedoms that individuals in the UK have access to.

They include:

- right to life
- freedom from torture and inhuman or degrading treatment
- right to liberty and security
- freedom from slavery and forced labour
- right to a fair trial
- no punishment without law
- respect for your private and family life, home and correspondence
- freedom of thought, belief and religion
- freedom of expression
- freedom of assembly and association
- right to marry and start a family
- protection from discrimination in respect of these rights and freedoms
- right to peaceful enjoyment of your property
- right to education
- right to participate in free elections.

For more on the Human Rights Act
The Ministry of Justice has produced a range of publications about the Act, including an Easy-Read booklet explaining what the Act means:
Ⓦ www.justice.gov.uk/human-rights

Mental Health (Discrimination) Act 2013

This UK Act of Parliament was passed after four MPs talked about their own experience of mental health conditions – the first time such a debate had happened in the House of Commons. It was introduced to the House of Commons by Gavin Barwell, Conservative MP for Croydon Central.

It stripped away historic discrimination debarring people with mental health conditions from public roles – from being a member of the UK parliament, the Scottish Parliament, the Welsh Assembly and the Northern Ireland Assembly, to being a company director to doing jury service.

The bill had the simple but vital aim: 'to remove the last significant form of discrimination in law in our society'.

The Act removes previous discriminatory legislation which suggests that people with mental health conditions can never recover and cannot be trusted to participate in social, political or economic life.

Disability Rights UK believes discriminatory mental health laws remain – allowing unfair compulsory detention and treatment – but this 2013 Act was a landmark.

To find UK legislation
You can read the Mental Health (Discrimination) Act, and find other UK legislation online.
Ⓦ www.legislation.gov.uk

Hate crime and harassment
LEGISLATION

Safety and security and the right to live free from fear and harassment are basic human rights.

Under the Criminal Justice Act 2003, when any criminal act is motivated by hostility on grounds of disability, this is viewed as an aggravating factor. This means a higher sentence can be passed.

> Under section 146 of the Criminal Justice Act sentencing can be tougher if a hate crime motive is established.

Although one in four people with a disability or long-term health condition are at some stage the victims of hate crime, there is in fact no legal definition of a disability hate crime. However, the Crown Prosecution Service (CPS) when it prosecutes cases of disability hate crime, the police and policy documents on dealing with such cases, use the following definition:

Any criminal offence, which is perceived, by the victim or any other person, to be motivated by hostility or prejudice based on a person's disability or perceived disability.

The Crown Prosecution Service

When a crime is motivated by hostility in this way, it should by law be taken more seriously and may be punished more severely than it otherwise would be.

To find out more about the CPS guidance on disability hate crime:
- Ⓦ www.cps.gov.uk/publications/ prosecution/disability.html

BULLYING OR DISABILITY-RELATED HARASSMENT OR CRIME

Abuse, violence, theft and neglect are all crimes, and if violence or abuse involves an element of hostility to someone because of disability, it can be classed as 'disability hate crime'.

In the past many people thought that because they had a disability or health condition no one would do anything, and often that was the case. But now police and the CPS are better trained and need you to report so they can act.

So if you believe that you are the victim of any criminal incident which happens because you are disabled it should be reported as a hate crime. If you or someone you know is facing violence, abuse or neglect it's vital to tell the police, your local disability organisation, or the council. Your local disability organisation should also be able to offer support. By reporting it, you can protect yourself and help the local police tackle hate crime more effectively.

If you don't feel confident talking to the police, seek support from a friend, family member or local disability organisation.

> Disability Rights UK has produced guidance for anyone experiencing harassment or hate crime, together with a guide for friends and relatives. *Let's Stop Disability Hate Crime* is available to download from the *How we can help* section of our website.
> Ⓦ www.disabilityrightsuk.org

REPORTING HATE CRIME

Centres to support people who have experienced disability-related harassment are opening around the country. One example is Blackpool Disability First.

Ⓦ www.disabilityfirst.org

Hidden in Plain Sight

In 2012, the EHRC held an Inquiry into disability-related harassment. The Inquiry's report, *Hidden in Plain Sight*, found that harassment of disabled people is a serious problem that needs to be better understood.

It discovered that the harassment cases that reach the courts are just the tip of the iceberg and that, for many, harassment is a commonplace experience.

Many people don't report harassment – because they don't know whom to report it to or fear the consequences of doing so – and there is a culture of disbelief surrounding harassment and bullying.

Worryingly, the Commission found that public authorities have failed to recognise the extent and impact of harassment and abuse of disabled people, to take action to prevent it happening in the first place and failed to intervene effectively.

The report made a number of recommendations and since 2012 there has been a more proactive and positive approach to reports of disability-related harassment.

Remember, harassment can be lots of little, apparently minor incidents that assume significance because they build up, because they are hurtful or because they make you feel afraid. While this can be particularly difficult for those with a pre-existing mental health condition, harassment can generate depression and anxiety in anyone. Seek help as soon as possible.

What can I report?

You can report any incident you believe was motivated by hostility based on your:

- health or disability
- race
- religion/belief
- sexual orientation
- transgender identity.

These incidents may involve physical attacks, verbal abuse, domestic abuse, harassment, damage to your property, bullying or graffiti.

Why report a hate crime or incident?

It's important to report hate crimes and incidents of harassment. By reporting them, you will enable the police, local councils and housing associations to build up patterns of behaviour locally and to highlight areas of concern within your community.

The Disability Hate Crime Network is a group of disabled people, charities and official bodies, including the police and CPS, who share news and information and work together to challenge and stop hate crime against disabled people.

Ⓦ www.dhcn.info

Just as importantly you can get the support you may need and help ensure that offenders are brought to justice.

Hate crimes and incidents hurt. They can be confusing and frightening. By reporting them when they happen to you, you may be able to prevent these incidents from happening to someone else or to you in the future.

In Lancashire, joint work by disabled people's organisations (DPOs) and agencies including the police and Crown Prosecution Service has led to increased confidence to report hate crimes and harassment.

With support from the Ministry of Justice, Blackpool's Disability First set up a Hate Crime and Incidents Reporting Centre.

It is increasing the confidence of people with health conditions and disabilities in reporting by going to a third-party reporting centre where they are supported by volunteers who also have health conditions and/or disabilities in a safe and secure environment.

There has also been training for 3000 frontline police officers to respond to crimes as 'hate crimes'.

This collaboration between DPOs and statutory agencies has led to a significant increase in reporting in Lancashire: from 64 reports of disability hate crime in 2012-13 to 172 in 2013-14.

HOW TO REPORT A HATE CRIME

There are several ways you can report a hate crime, whether you have been a victim, a witness, or you are reporting on behalf of someone else. Start by talking to someone you trust: if you decide to go to the police, you could ask that person to come with you.

1: In an emergency

Call 999 or 112. If you cannot make voice calls, you can now contact the 999 emergency services by SMS text from your mobile phone. To use this text service you need to first register with emergencySMS.
ⓦ www.emergencysms.org.uk

2: Contact the police

You can speak to them in confidence. You do not have to give your personal details, but please be aware the investigation and ability to prosecute the offender(s) is severely limited if the police cannot contact you. Contact your local police force, either by telephone or by visiting your local police station. Details on how to contact your local police force can be found at:
ⓦ www.police.uk

Taking charge

Campaigning for better communication
After lobbying by deaf people, Merseyside Police introduced a system which allows deaf people and people with hearing impairments to contact them and to report incidents to the control rooms by using mobile phone texting technology.

3: Report online
You can report online using the facility on this website. Go to the 'Reporting online' page:
- Ⓦ www.report-it.org.uk/your_police_force

4: Self-reporting form
You can download the self-reporting form and send this to your local police force. The form, including an Easy Read version, can be found on the 'Report a hate crime' page:
- Ⓦ www.report-it.org.uk

Steven is 27 and has cerebral palsy. He has a job, looks after himself and lives in his own home with some support.

To get to work Steven takes a bus, where he is often called names and bullied by schoolchildren. They've messed up his hair, poured cans of drink over his head and even put out a cigarette on his coat. He didn't tell anyone for a long time but his support worker became worried as Steven started to become depressed and frightened.

Together they decided to report what was happening to the police and Steven got help from Victim Support. There has been support from neighbourhood police, and support for the bus company to stop hate crimes happening. There have also been projects in the school to help pupils understand that no one should be treated badly because they are different.

5: Third-party reporting centres
Third party disability hate crime reporting centres, run by people with health conditions and disabilities, are beginning to open up around the country to support people who are experiencing harassment on grounds of a health condition or disability. They can report the incident with you or on your behalf. You can report to someone who understands disability – and will help you with the whole process.

Disability Rights UK is working with a number of areas to develop these centres. In other areas local agencies, such as the Citizens Advice bureau and Community Voluntary Services can report the incident on your behalf and provide you with advice and support.

6: Crimestoppers
If you do not want to talk to the police or fill in the reporting forms, you can still report a hate crime by calling Crimestoppers or via their website. You do not have to give your name and what you say is confidential. It is free to call.
- ☎ 0800 555111
- Ⓦ www.crimestoppers-uk.org

"Me and my wife got help from the council to leave our previous home following a spate of disability hate crime incidents. We now feel safe and are near to my wife's family. After the incidents happened, we had to live apart for three years until a suitable property became available – that was a huge strain. But we are together again now. We feel safe and secure."

Challenging discrimination at work

Pat worked in further education, mainly with students needing additional support. The work was challenging and Pat's role expanded as demand for the service was high. This created a very pressurised role and Pat asked for an assistant or a change in some of her duties. She felt that if she was required to take on the wide range of duties within the role, then the post should be re-graded.

She told her manager that she had mental health problems (depression) and that her condition was deteriorating, partly because of the stress involved in the job. The manager's response was that the whole service was under strain and everyone had to work harder than they would like. Pat felt unsupported and that her mental wellbeing was affected. She became unwell and took time off work.

Pat's health began to improve and she felt that she was almost able to return. Then an opportunity came up for a similar job in a different organisation. Worried that returning to her old job would cause her health to deteriorate again, she decided to resign.

Pat decided to get advice about her legal rights and whether her old employer had been treating her fairly, so that she would know what to do if similar things happened in her new job. She had been invited to an exit interview by her employer, who may well have been concerned that she intended to claim constructive dismissal or discrimination.

Mind's Legal Unit helped Pat to summarise her concerns and explained how the law should have worked. It was likely that Pat had been discriminated against for two reasons: Her manager had been less sympathetic about her health concerns than she had been about colleagues with physical illnesses and hadn't considered making reasonable adjustments to help Pat. She considered starting a discrimination claim but knew she would find this stressful and time-consuming and she wanted to save her energies for her new job. So she decided to use the exit interview to make sure that her former employer understood her experiences, so that others would be treated better in future.

Pat felt that her former employer took a lot of her points on board, which was her main intention in going to the exit interview. She was surprised when they offered her a payment similar to the upgrade in salary she had been asking for (without admitting that they had done anything wrong).

Mind ensured that Pat got independent legal advice about what to do next – if she accepted the payment, her employer wanted her to sign a compromise agreement so she would not be able to change her mind and bring a discrimination or unfair dismissal claim. Pat decided to accept the payment – happy that she had been able to put her points across effectively. She says that former colleagues are now reporting a more understanding attitude from senior management.

You can give as little or as much personal information as you wish. With your details the incident can be investigated fully and you can get the service you deserve and the support you need. Without your details the report will be used for monitoring purposes to get a true vision of what is happening.

Stop Hate UK works to challenge all forms of hate crime and discrimination, based on any aspect of an individual's identity. They provide independent, confidential and accessible reporting and support for victims, witnesses and third parties and offer a range of other services including training, education and consultancy. Their core activities also include awareness-raising, campaigning and delivering projects on a variety of issues related to hate crime and equality.

Stop Hate UK provides a hate crime reporting service for a number of areas in the UK (check their website for details):
- Ⓦ www.stophateuk.org/report-hate-crime

24-hour helpline for learning disability hate crimes across England and Wales:
- Ⓣ 0808 802 1155
- Ⓦ www.stophateuk.org/report-learning-disability-hate-crime

To connect to an online British Sign Language (BSL) interpreter:
- Ⓦ www.signtranslate-002.com

CHALLENGING BULLYING AT WORK

Bullying or harassment at work can leave you feeling intimidated, embarrassed and depressed. Bullying behaviour could include anything from spreading malicious rumours to being continually undermined or denied training or promotion. Harassment is against the law.

The first thing to do is to see if you can resolve the situation internally by speaking to your manager, HR or trade union representative. If this doesn't work you have the right to be able to lodge a complaint under your employer's grievance procedure. If this doesn't work you can take your complaint to an employment tribunal.

Many people say that being discriminated against in work and social situations can be a bigger burden than the illness itself.
Time to Change Campaign

ACAS may be able to help you and you can get free advice by calling their helpline. See contacts at the end of this chapter.

ACAS has also produced a guidance leaflet on bullying or harassment:
- Ⓦ www.acas.org.uk/CHttpHandler.ashx?id=306&p=0

The Equality Advice Support Service or your local law centre may also be able to help.

Victim Support can offer you help and advice in coping with the effects of crime, practical support, like getting locks changed or filling in forms, advice on dealing with the police. They can also help you if you think you want to pursue your concerns in the courts.

Ⓦ www.victimsupport.org.uk

Bullying UK offers help and advice about bullying at work and also to parents and families of children with disabilities who are concerned about bullying.

Ⓦ www.bullying.co.uk

"I am a manager of a small team. I have a visual impairment. I found out from a new colleague that members of my team had been writing rude things about me and sticking them on the back of my chair. They would whisper and laugh when I came into the office. I challenged them and they said I had no sense of humour – the 'fun' went on.

Eventually, I went off sick for a while. My union rep contacted me and came with me to a number of meetings with my manager and my team. I was able to explain how much their behaviour had affected me and a bit about what it is like to have a visual impairment – how it can make you feel left out, particularly in a big open plan office because you can't pick up on visual cues. I think the people harassing me were quite shocked. One of them came to me privately and told me how awful she felt. The problem's stopped now."

In 2012 a former soldier blinded by an IRA bomb was awarded £200,000 compensation by an employment tribunal after it found he had been bullied at work. The tribunal in Cardiff ruled that Andrew Bull had also been harassed and eventually lost his job at Blaenau Gwent council due to his disability.

There are other forms of bullying and abuse, including financial.

Legal advice and support
Equality and Human Rights Commission (EHRC)

Parliament set up the Commission to challenge discrimination, and to protect and promote human rights.

The EHRC has produced a series of guides to explain your rights in employment.

Ⓦ www.equalityhumanrights.com/ your-rights/employment/guidance-workers

The EHRC also explains the rights you have in relation to buying things and using services.

Ⓦ www.equalityhumanrights.com/ advice-and-guidance/service-users-guidance

For information or to contact EHRC: Correspondence Unit, Arndale House, The Arndale Centre, Manchester M4 3AQ

Ⓔ correspondence@ equalityhumanrights.com

Ⓦ www.equalityhumanrights.com/ about-us

Equality Advisory Support Service (EASS)
If you need expert information, advice and support on discrimination and human rights issues and law that could help you, especially if you need more help than advice agencies and other local organisations can provide, contact the Equality Advisory & Support Service.

FREEPOST Equality Advisory Support Service FPN4431
- 📞 0808 800 0082; textphone 0808 800 0084
- 🌐 www.equalityadvisoryservice.com

ACAS
The Advisory, Conciliation and Arbitration Service (ACAS) is an independent service funded by the government which aims to improve our working lives through better employment relations.

If you think you might have been discriminated against at work, ACAS can give you independent advice and may be able to help you resolve a problem with an employer.

You can get free advice from the ACAS website or by calling their helpline:
- 📞 Helpline 0300 123 1100
  Open Monday-Friday, 8am-8pm and Saturday, 9am-1pm
  Text Relay 18001 0300 123 1100
- 🌐 www.acas.org.uk

TRADE UNIONS
You may be a member of a trade union, which will offer help, advice and representation for you and other members at work, or across the sector you work in.

A union can provide you with advice, support and legal help if you are concerned you have been treated unfairly at work. Some unions offer additional welfare, emotional or financial advice and services if you are having problems at home.

There are more than 50 recognised trade unions in the UK. To help you find the right union for your area of employment:
- 🌐 www.tuc.org.uk/britains-unions

Staying in work
Susan Archibald lives in Fife with her husband and four children. Previously a street sweeper, she developed a mobility impairment after unsuccessful surgery. Endless barriers to getting a job on attempting to rejoin the workforce prompted Susan to take her employer, Fife Council, to court.

The case went on for five years. Susan tells of having to crawl up a spiral staircase five days in a row to attend a disability discrimination hearing at one ironic stage in the battle.

Supported by the Disability Rights Commission (whose functions are now delivered by the EHRC, she finally won in 2004. The judgment subsequently changed UK employment laws for disabled workers, putting a duty on employers to consider redeployment as a reasonable adjustment if an employee becomes unable to do their job due to disability.

Shaping your own career

Alex, 42, has been in a wheelchair since he was seven. He says that most of his experiences at work have been good, although some companies still have a long way to go.

"I attended a mainstream school so I have never thought of myself as different or even disabled. Yes, some things are a little harder for me, but with a little bit of thought and some adaptations I can manage to do most things an able-bodied person could. When I left school I started working in IT. My first employer was very forward thinking for the time and made a great effort to make sure that all my needs were met and that I wasn't treated any differently from any other employee. I am very glad that they were my first experience of the workplace as it allowed me to see what is possible.

In my late 20s I was looking for a bit of a change and got a job as an IT training manager in a small company. As soon as I started, I realised that it was a mistake. I think they took me on because they needed to show they had filled their quota of disabled people rather than actually wanting me there. Nothing was set up conveniently for me and it was a constant challenge to get things changed. I found myself excluded from certain meetings because wheelchair access was impossible and had decisions made over my head. Eventually I took them to an employment tribunal and won, which was a good boost to my confidence."

Alex says that he is happy that discrimination is now taken seriously but people's attitudes need to change if disabled people are going to be treated equally.

"Apart from that one company I have always been treated well by my employers but you still have to face some ignorance from colleagues.

I think all companies need to offer training about dealing with disability and help promote understanding and acceptance in the workplace. That is what I do now. I have set up my own company which I never dreamed of when I was younger. Companies all across the country bring me and my team in to run training sessions and it is very satisfying. Attitudes have definitely changed and as the younger generation come into the workplace I think it will only get better.

No disabled person should ever feel that they have to settle for sub-standard facilities or unfair treatment. If they are capable of doing the job as well as their colleagues then they should be given the same opportunities.

Laws have definitely helped but I think that individuals also need to take responsibility for their own treatment. If you feel that you are being discriminated against then don't be afraid to speak up. Employers must be accountable for their actions and you need to make sure that you are judged by your ability not your disability."

The umbrella body for all unions, the TUC (Trades Union Congress), has further information on how a union might be able to help you on its website.
Ⓦ www.tuc.org.uk/equality-issues

Remember, if you are unable to do your existing job after acquiring a health condition or disability, your employer may have a duty, as a reasonable adjustment, to redeploy you.

SUPPORT ORGANISATIONS
Many disability and health organisations may be able to offer support if you experience discrimination.

Time to Change
The Time to Change campaign is challenging stigma and discrimination against people with mental health conditions, thanks to the work of two big UK charities, Mind and Rethink. The campaign debunks the myths that lead to prejudice and stigma about mental health issues. It shows that when people with and without mental health problems have contact with each other – working or living together –that breaks down prejudice. It also shows that it is often the reaction from those we are closest to that we fear the most.

The campaign encourages people with mental health conditions to talk openly about their experiences, and asks us all to pledge to talk to and support those who need it without prejudice.
Ⓦ www.time-to-change.org.uk

Where to get advice
FACE TO FACE ADVICE AND CASE WORK

Citizens Advice
The Citizens Advice service aims to help people resolve a variety of problems by providing free, independent and confidential advice.

To find a CAB in your area (England and Wales) visit:
Ⓦ www.citizensadvice.org.uk/index/getadvice.htm

To find a CAB in Scotland visit:
Ⓦ www.cas.org.uk/bureaux

CAB is also developing a national phone service. If it is not yet available in your area, you will hear options for recorded information.

For England:
Ⓣ 08444 111 444
For Wales:
Ⓣ 08444 77 20 20
TextRelay users should call:
Ⓣ 08444 111 445

Tackling fraud
In May 2014, a disabled pensioner who lost more than £700,000 in a telesales scam won most of his money back after taking his case to court. The High Court heard that 77-year-old David Parker, who is hard of hearing, has cerebral palsy and uses a wheelchair, was 'cajoled, bullied and, on occasions lied to' in order to get him to part with his retirement savings as part of a 'land banking' scheme by cold callers.

Law centres

Law centres are not-for-profit legal practices providing free legal advice and representation to disadvantaged people. There are around 50 Law Centres in England, Wales and Northern Ireland, staffed by solicitors and barristers who specialise in areas of civil law including employment, housing, discrimination, welfare benefits, education and immigration.

To find your nearest Law Centre:
In England, Wales and Northern Ireland:
Ⓦ www.lawcentres.org.uk

In Scotland:
Ⓦ www.scotlawcentres.blogspot.co.uk

Legal aid

Legal aid can help pay for legal advice, family mediation or representation in court or at a tribunal. Legal aid is different in England and Wales compared to Scotland and to Northern Ireland.

You can get guidance on your eligibility from the Civil Legal Advice gateway:
Ⓣ 0845 345 4 345;
   textphone 0845 609 6677
Ⓦ www.gov.uk/community-legal-advice

If you are eligible, you may be able to get help with legal aid for:
- benefit appeals
- debt, if your home is at risk
- special educational needs
- housing
- discrimination issues
- help and advice if you're a victim of domestic violence
- issues around a child being taken into care.

PHONE HELPLINES

Age UK

Age UK provides advice and information to older people via its adviceline:
Ⓣ 0800 169 6565
Ⓦ www.ageuk.org.uk

Carers UK

Carers UK provides advice and information to carers via its adviceline:
Ⓣ 0808 808 7777
Ⓦ www.carersuk.org

Civil Legal Advice (CLA)

Get free and confidential legal advice in England and Wales if you're eligible for legal aid. Check if you can get legal aid to see if you're eligible for free advice.
Ⓦ www.gov.uk/check-legal-aid

Online enquiry form
Ⓣ 0845 345 4345;
   textphone 0845 609 6677

You can ask Civil Legal Advice for a free call back – use the online service or text 'legalaid' and your name to 80010. There's a free translation service if English isn't your first language. You can also talk to Civil Legal Advice by booking a British Sign Language interpreter.

DIAL

There are around 120 local Disability Information and Advice Line services (DIALs) throughout Great Britain run by and for disabled people.

To find out if there is a DIAL that covers your area:
Ⓣ 0808 800 3333
Ⓦ www.scope.org.uk/support/disabled-people/local-advice

Disability Law Service

Disability Law Service provides specialist legal advice for disabled people, their families and carers on community care and employment.

- **T** 020 7791 9800
- **W** www.dls.org.uk

Disability Rights UK

We operate several advice lines. Check our website for helpline opening hours or email anytime.

Disabled Students Helpline

This line provides advice to disabled students who are studying in England. We can support students who are studying in Wales and Scotland with general information on the Equality Act, welfare benefits and access to Higher Education. We also provide advice on post-16 education, training and apprenticeship and welcome enquiries from disabled students or professionals working with disabled students.

- **T** 0800 328 5050
- **E** students@disabilityrightsuk.org

We recommend that disabled students who wish to study in Scotland contact Lead Scotland for more specialised information and advice about education and training in Scotland.

- **T** 0131 228 9441
- **E** info@lead.org.uk

For more about our helplines

You can find out more about our public helplines and resources for members in the *How we can help* section of our website.

- **W** www.disabilityrightsuk.org

Self Directed Support Line

This line provides advice on:
- individual budgets, personalisation and direct payments
- funding from social services in relation to a disabled person's care needs and advice on appealing against decisions
- employing personal assistants.

- **T** 0300 555 1525
- **E** selfdirectedsupport@ disabilityrightsuk.org

Equality Advisory Support Service

The Equality Advisory Support Service (EASS) is a government funded helpline that replaced the Equality and Human Rights Commission (EHRC) Helpline. It is provided by Sitel who are working with Disability Rights UK, the Law Centres Federation, Voiceability, the British Institute of Human Rights and the Royal Association for Deaf People.

The helpline advises on issues relating to equality and human rights, across England, Scotland and Wales. Any individual who has a discrimination or human rights related issue can contact the service, which also takes referrals from organisations that, due to capacity or funding issues, are unable to provide the required support. The service is not available to employers or service providers.

EASS explains legal rights and remedies within discrimination legislation, describes options for informal resolution and helps people to pursue them. It can refer people to conciliation or mediation services.

The service does not provide legal advice. It can help people who need or want to seek a legal solution by helping to establish eligibility for legal aid and if they are not eligible, to find an accessible legal service or to prepare and lodge a claim themselves.

EASS works collaboratively with the organisations from whom it receives referrals and, where the individual consents, lets them know the outcome of cases they refer. It works closely with EHRC, referring on potential test cases and sharing information to inform the EHRC's wider work on equality.

Equality Advisory & Support Service (EASS)
FREEPOST Equality Advisory Support Service FPN4431
- 📞 0808 800 0082;
  textphone 0808 800 0084
  Open 9am to 8pm Monday to Friday
  and 10am to 2pm Saturday
  Closed on Sundays and Bank Holidays
- 🌐 www.equalityadvisoryservice.com

There is a webcam portal for BSL users via the Royal Association for Deaf people.

Irwin Mitchell
Irwin Mitchell is one of the UK's largest law firms with offices across the country. They offer legal aid to eligible applicants. They have experience of all types of legal cases and have taken cases all the way to the Supreme Court, European Court of Justice and the European Court of Human Rights when necessary.

To get in touch with a member of the Public Law team at Irwin Mitchell, contact Alex Rook:
- 📞 0870 1500 100
- ✉ publiclawnewenquiries@
  irwinmitchell.com
- 🌐 www.irwinmitchell.com/personal/
  administrative-public-law

Public Law Project
The Public Law Project is a national legal charity. They run a telephone advice line on civil legal aid. The line is aimed at advisers with queries about the civil legal aid regime under the Legal Aid, Sentencing and Punishment of Offenders Act 2012, which came into force on 1 April 2013. The advice line will cover all legal aid issues arising under LASPOA, including exceptional funding, scope, means and the Telephone Gateway.
- 📞 0808 165 0170 (free to callers)
- 🌐 www.publiclawproject.org.uk

Shelter
Has a national telephone advice line staffed by trained housing advisers.
- 📞 0808 800 4444
- 🌐 http://england.shelter.org.uk
  http://scotland.shelter.org.uk

Unity Law
Unity Law are specialist equality discrimination and occupational disease lawyers. If you are being treated less favourably because of your disability in work (or in seeking work), Unity Law may be able to help.
- 📞 0114 361 0000
- ✉ info@unity-law.co.uk
- 🌐 www.unity-law.co.uk

ON THE WEB

Adviceguide

Citizens Advice provides online information on your rights, including benefits, housing, family matters and employment, and on debt, consumer and legal issues.

ⓦ www.adviceguide.org.uk

Advicelocal

Advicelocal is an online service covering all 33 London boroughs. The site offers access to welfare law, housing, debt and social care topics and includes a searchable database – advicefinder – of over 1500 organisations, offering advice or information services at either a borough level, across all of London or nationally.

ⓦ http://advicelocal.org.uk

Legal Aid Agency – Community Legal Advice

This is an online database which enables you to search for legal advisers or solicitors near you.

ⓦ http://find-legal-advice.justice.gov.uk

ADVICE REFERRAL

Bar Pro Bono Unit

The Bar Pro Bono Unit can put people who need legal advice and representation in touch with barristers who are willing to work for no fee or 'pro bono' ('for the good'). The Unit takes applications through advice agencies and solicitors and aims to help in cases where someone cannot afford to pay, cannot get legal aid and has a 'meritorious' case (in other words, a good case).

ⓦ www.barprobono.org.uk

Free Representation Unit

The Free Representation Unit (FRU) is a registered charity. It can provide legal advice, case preparation and advocacy in tribunal cases in all areas of social security law. Cases must be referred to the FRU through a referral agency. Some of these are listed on the FRU website and they include Citizens Advice Bureaux and Law Centres and some solicitors. The FRU cannot accept referrals direct from members of the public and it does not accept cases until a tribunal hearing date has been arranged.

ⓦ www.thefru.org.uk

Making a complaint
HOUSING

If you want to make a complaint about housing, you should first complain to your landlord. If you do not feel that your complaint has been dealt with, register it with the Housing Ombudsman. Local council tenants should contact the Local Government Ombudsman. The Housing Ombudsman operates only in England.

Housing Ombudsman

81 Aldwych, London WC2B 4HN

ⓣ 0300 111 3000
ⓔ info@housing-ombudsman.org.uk
ⓦ www.housing-ombudsman.org.uk

The Housing Ombudsman is an independent organisation that can take up complaints from residents of housing provided by social landlords, including those who have taken over properties from councils.

GOODS AND SERVICES

If you want to complain about a business, start off by making an informal complaint face to face or over the phone.

- Plan and write down what you want to say in advance.
- Try running through what you want to say with someone else first.
- Stay calm. You're more likely to get sidetracked if you get annoyed.
- Keep a record of the date and time of all conversations, and whom you dealt with.

Many service providers will have formal complaints procedures. Try to find out what the organisation's complaints procedure is and follow it. If it doesn't seem to have one, put your complaint in writing. Make sure you keep a copy of the letter. You should send it by recorded delivery so you have proof the service provider received it.

COMPLAINING TO A REGULATORY OR MEMBERSHIP BODY

Some organisations belong to membership bodies. Part of the role of a membership organisation is to ensure that its members' services meet certain standards.

You could think about reporting the organisation discriminating against you to one of these bodies. They won't usually be able to pay you compensation but they might be able to investigate your complaint and stop the organisation from behaving like that in the future.

If you have a complaint about a local authority, you should make your complaint directly to them. If you do not get a satisfactory resolution, you can take your complaint to the Local Government Ombudsman.
ⓦ www.lgo.org.uk/making-a-complaint

The Equality and Human Rights Commission has guidance on considering which process to follow depending on the nature of your complaint.
ⓦ www.equalityhumanrights.com/your-rights/equal-rights/using-your-rights/deciding-whether-to-make-a-claim

The Equality Advisory Support Service and the Citizens Advice Bureau can advise you on how to pursue a complaint about discrimination.

You may want to consider taking your complaint to the county court, in which case you will need legal advice.

The Law Centres Network set up across parts of the UK can provide you with impartial legal advice.
ⓦ www.lawcentres.org.uk

You could also talk to a consumer programme such as Radio Four's 'You and Yours' or speak to your MP.

Disability Rights UK has additional advice on your rights and how to make a complaint. You can find all our factsheets in the *How we can help* section of our website;
ⓦ www.disabilityrightsuk.org